UNIFORM SYSTEM
OF
ACCOUNTS FOR RESTAURANTS

Fourth Revised Edition
1968

ADOPTED AND RECOMMENDED BY
THE NATIONAL RESTAURANT ASSOCIATION

Prepared by
LAVENTHOL KREKSTEIN HORWATH & HORWATH

Including
RECORD KEEPING FOR THE SMALL RESTAURANT

Seventh Printing 1979

ISBN 0-914528-00-9

MG-936

TABLE OF CONTENTS

INDEX TO EXHIBITS
AND SPECIAL SECTIONS OF TEXT

PAGE

PART II
EXAMPLES OF RESTAURANT FINANCIAL STATEMENTS

PART III
RECORD KEEPING FOR THE SMALL RESTAURANT

APPENDIX A

APPENDIX B

PREFACE

The Board of Directors of the National Restaurant Association is gratified that the book, "Uniform System of Accounts for Restaurants," published in 1958, has proven over the years to be the Association's "Best Seller." More important, this continuing demand has been evidence that its membership has responded well to the assistance this publication has given to restaurant operators in the area of creating a common language for the industry based on an intelligent means of analyzing their results. It also has given wider opportunity to restaurant owners and operators to benefit by comparison of their figures with those of others in the business and with the published results of restaurant studies made by the Association itself, the trade press, colleges, accounting firms and others.

There have been marked changes in over-all restaurant facilities, which have responded to changes in the traveling pattern of the public. These, in turn, are brought about largely by the decentralization of metropolitan areas and the accessibility of restaurants to new markets created by the ease of travel by automobile and airplane. Customer demand and desires have also changed in ways that have influenced the shifting of markets for restaurant volume, have created the need for new facilities and, in some instances, rendered others obsolete. The concurrent development of super highways, airport facilities, suburban shopping areas, vacation and resort spots, in-plant and institutional feeding have all contributed to this change.

On the expense side, the inclusion as of February 1, 1967 of the restaurant business under the Fair Labor Standards Act, commonly called the "Wage and Hour Law," has made payroll reporting and controls a more important factor than heretofore. The improvements in equipment, the development of convenience foods and other similar advances in operating methods have also now begun to show their influence on operating results.

Aware of these changes and developments, the Directors of the Association have determined that, in order to keep pace with them, it is now advisable to again revise the "Uniform System of Accounts for Restaurants." They, accordingly, authorized the accounting firm of Laventhol Krekstein Horwath & Horwath, who had prepared the previous editions published under the auspices of the National Restaurant Association in 1930, 1942 and 1958, to work out this fourth revised edition. This work was again supervised and edited under the direction of Mr. G. O. Podd, C.P.A., a partner of this firm, assisted by Mr. Earl Felske, C.P.A., and Mr. Kenneth Burley, M.A.S., of their Chicago office.

The Board of Directors therefore adopted the following resolution at their meeting in Chicago on May 21, 1967:

"RESOLVED, that the NATIONAL RESTAURANT ASSOCIATION adopts and recommends to its membership the UNIFORM SYSTEM OF ACCOUNTS FOR RESTAURANTS as revised in 1968 and that it be made available for sale and distribution by the Association; and RESOLVED, that such UNIFORM SYSTEM OF ACCOUNTS FOR RESTAURANTS, fourth revised edition, be copyrighted in the name of the Association."

The objectives of the Board in adopting this resolution are to bring the statement presentation and terminology up to date in accordance with the latest trends in business and accounting and to continue to promote a uniform arrangement of financial statements and a common language that can be used by all restaurants regardless of their size or type.

In keeping with the demand by restaurant operators for authentic data on operating results and guidance on their financial problems, this issue has followed the pattern used in 1958 and again contains detailed explanations of the suggested classification of accounts and the presentation of samples of both profit and loss statements and statements of financial condition (balance sheets), illustrating its practicability and use.

While it is thus, in fact, a veritable textbook for the restaurant operator on the subject of restaurant accounting, its primary objective is to help the operator of the smaller restaurant to interpret his results and financial position and at the same time give due consideration to the manner in which the Uniform System can be used to advantage by the large restaurant.

It is the hope of the Board of Directors that the membership of the National Restaurant Association will continue to benefit from the general adoption of The Uniform System of Accounts for Restaurants in their own operations and, as a corollary, from the wealth of reliable data available for comparison with their operations that will result from the future studies and published figures based on its use.

Respectively submitted,
DONALD GREENAWAY
Executive Vice President
NATIONAL RESTAURANT ASSOCIATION

BOARD OF DIRECTORS
NATIONAL RESTAURANT ASSOCIATION

Gentlemen:

We express our appreciation of the assignment to prepare this, the fourth revised edition of the Uniform System of Accounts for Restaurants, for publication by the National Restaurant Association.

In preparing the text and illustrative exhibits contained in this edition, we have reviewed a large number of financial statements of restaurants of all types and sizes in various areas of the United States.

We have also considered the changes in restaurant operations and the related problems which have become evident as influences in the statement presentation and interpretation since the 1958 text was prepared. We have, of course, also reviewed the previous editions of the Uniform System of Accounts for Restaurants and other published works on the subject of restaurant accounting.

In this connection, we also want to express our appreciation to Mr. Donald Greenaway, Executive Vice President of The National Restaurant Association, your executive staff, and the members of your Association for their cooperation and advice in compiling this revised text.

Although you will note that the general pattern of the classification of accounts and illustrative statements has not changed from that of the previous edition, which we believe has proven its practical application to the restaurant business, there are the following few instances in which they have been updated and these should be mentioned at the outset:

1. Changes in the classification of accounts are minor as compared to the 1958 text. An explanation more clearly outlining the reasons for calculating employees' meals and the payroll record requirements on such meal credits under the Fair Labor Standards Act was added to the text on "Food Cost."

2. Because of the Wage and Hour Law, some restaurants are considering the adoption of the policy of making service charges in lieu of tips and are changing their payroll records accordingly. This practice, however, has not become widespread, and in order to retain the validity of comparisons with restaurants that do not have such a policy, the items of service charges and their distribution are shown separately in the Uniform System. This is similar to the treatment used for the cost of employees' meals.

3. In the "Payroll Schedule," Schedule A-4, the classification was augmented by adding a line each for the personnel and payroll office, data processing payroll and gardener's payroll.

In the "Direct Operating Expenses," Schedule A-6, a line has been added for employees' transportation, which is an item in some drive-in and outlying restaurants.

In the "Administrative and General," Schedule A-10, a line has been added for data-processing costs and one for personnel expenses.

The lines for Federal Cabaret Taxes and Admissions have been eliminated as these taxes are no longer being levied.

4. The major changes, which resulted in a complete revision of the example statements in Part II of this book, were made in order to bring their figures closer to current operating results and, to some extent, to reflect the effect of increased payroll costs on the operating ratios and of credit-card acceptance on the balance sheet.

9

You will note that the ratios in the examples shown in Part II are a far cry from the percentages considered normal in years back when we talked of a 25% payroll and a 40% food cost, at which time no portion of the income dollar was taken by employee benefit expenses.

5. Examples of financial statements were added for "drive-in" restaurants in Exhibits K and L.

6. An example of an annual study of restaurant operations has also been included as Appendix C.

7. In Part III, "Record Keeping for the Small Restaurant," forms for a weekly payroll sheet and employment card were added to assist in outlining what is believed to be the record keeping necessary to meet the requirements of the Wage and Hour Law. The purpose in this is to prepare the smaller restaurants in the event they come under the jurisdiction of the Fair Labor Standards Act.

It is realized that restaurants generally have just begun — as of February 1, 1967 — to come under its jurisdiction and that later experience with its requirements and with the regulations of the Wage and Hour Division of the Federal Labor Department — and in some instances with state laws and regulations as well — may change this suggested outline and form. Therefore they are not included as final, but rather as a guide dependent upon today's experience. They will, however, serve the purpose of at least alerting the operator to devise a method of meeting the record requirements of this law.

8. A brief description of the 1966 amendments to the Fair Labor Standards Act and the regulations thus far issued pertaining thereto as they relate to the service industries as of February 1, 1967 has been added as Appendix D.

The basic classification of accounts included in this edition again conforms to the major elements that make up the picture of operations and financial position, and it comprises a grouping of income and cost items in simple summary form that can be used by all restaurants, large and small. At the same time, this classification emphasizes the major components that portray the operation in a way that provides for intelligent analysis.

The more detailed items that make up each major classification are then listed and explained so that the restaurant man can expand or contract his accounts and statements to the extent he feels necessary or advisable to give him the complete information he may desire in analyzing his results.

The reader will note, in connection with the illustrative statements presented in this edition, how the details dovetail into the condensed summary statement and, conversely, how the simple condensed statement can be expanded almost indefinitely to meet his desires for detailed information. Thus, the flexibility of the Uniform System of Accounts for Restaurants is, we believe, amply demonstrated by the sample statements contained in Part II.

The question may, however, arise as to why this book does not also contain examples of statements for chain operations, in-plant feeding, department store restaurants, hotels, clubs, hospitals and other institutions.

Although a review of the statements made in making the decisions as to the examples to be used clearly indicated that most of these types of restaurant operations would fit into the Uniform System, many could use it only in part because of other considerations involved.

Many chain or multiple unit operators, for example, have a central commissary and administrative office, the costs and expenses of which must either be distributed in some fashion to the individual units or be considered as operating overhead after arriving at the profit contribution of each unit.

Department stores, hotels, clubs and hospitals have additional income producing departments which contribute to the support of their overhead and fixed costs.

In-plant feeding operations are often based on management contracts, sometimes subsidized by the establishment in which they are located, and thus also have a special problem with indirect costs which may lead them to use the Uniform System only to the extent of the direct sales and costs of the restaurant unit.

Also, in some hospitals and institutions the accounting must conform to the accounting system of the store, plant, or institution of which they are a part, often based on local government rules and regulations.

One illustration of this is included in Exhibit M, contained in Part II of this book, which shows the form of restaurant departmental operating statement under the Uniform System of Accounts for Hotels and Clubs.

In view of these differences in requirements, it would be difficult and confusing to attempt to outline variations in the Uniform System to meet the needs of all of these feeding operations. This text, therefore, deals with a Uniform System for restaurants in general with the idea that the types of operations just mentioned could also benefit from conforming to it insofar as is possible within the limitations of their own systems.

In substance, therefore, our major concern in this publication is admittedly the commercial restaurant which is a complete operation in itself, although the treatment of direct costs and expenses as outlined could also be useful, for comparative purposes, to other types of food operations that cannot conform completely to the Uniform System in its entirety.

Very truly yours,
LAVENTHOL KREKSTEIN HORWATH & HORWATH

PART I

UNIFORM SYSTEM OF ACCOUNTS FOR RESTAURANTS

This section outlines in considerable detail the classification of income and expense items dealt with in restaurant operation in accordance with the Uniform System of Accounts for Restaurants. The accounts which contain the figures for the Profit and Loss Statement are presented first, inasmuch as they are most likely to be of the greatest interest to the restaurant operator. These are followed by the Balance Sheet accounts which are included to make this presentation complete.

The primary purpose of the Uniform System is to give restaurant men generally, both large and small, a common language in connection with their accounting statements, so that when they discuss their business with each other they will know that each one is talking about the same thing when they mention such things as "food costs, payrolls, etc." At the same time, this common language must take the form that will give the vast majority of restaurant men a clear picture of the major elements of their business, showing how each major item contributes to it. By its use, restaurant men will not only have the benefit of the analytical interpretation and experience of accountants in the presentation of their own figures, but will also get an extra dividend in that they are put in a position to intelligently compare their operations with the statements of others in the restaurant business and with the vast quantity of published figures constantly being available to them through their trade associations, trade periodicals and special studies covering the restaurant field. Thus, as the Uniform System becomes more universally adopted, they can make these comparisons without having to make tedious adjustments of their own figures.

PROFIT AND LOSS STATEMENT

The profit and loss statement form recommended under the Uniform System of Accounts For Restaurants is flexible and can be readily adapted to the very small restaurant as well as to the large operations. The extent to which the restaurant man will show the details of his sales and expenses in his statements depends entirely on his own desires as to the information he wants them to portray. A profit and loss statement should, however, be sufficiently comprehensive to answer the questions that would normally arise in the conduct of his own business.

For this reason, the various elements of operation are summarized into their major logical groupings for the preparation of the basic statement, which may be amplified indefinitely.

Although an attempt has been made in this text to list as fully as possible the items that will come under each main heading, there will always be, in the practical application of the system, some types of income or expense that are not specifically mentioned. In such cases, unlisted items should be entered in the group that contains transactions similar in nature.

In some of the larger restaurants and in chain operations, the statement presentation may be complicated by the existence of a central commissary, bakery or executive office. In these instances, the apportionment of the costs of these central units to the restaurants involved is usually made by a method or formula which best suits those in charge of operations, and their book-keeping is designed on this particular basis. It would thus be difficult, if not impossible, to devise any uniform method of distribution for these central units that would satisfy all, since many of the distributions depend on the experience and judgment of the individual official in charge. No attempt has been made in this text to present any classifications for these central units, and the Uniform System as outlined provides only for the ultimate distribution of their costs to the retail operation of the restaurants themselves.

The form of profit and loss statement outlined in this section is recommended as a standard for the restaurant business. The text immediately following explains the reasoning used in arriving at this form, which is the result of the original intention to devise some uniform classification that would suit the needs of restaurants in general.

SALES

The basic element of restaurant operation is the sale of food and beverages, and all of the major items of cost and expense are viewed in their relationship to these sales. For this reason, the form of the statement of profit and loss adopted starts with a portrayal of food and beverage sales.

In the booklet, "RECORD KEEPING" issued by the National Restaurant Association in 1942, the profit and loss statement form showed the details of the cigar counter sales and costs on the face of the statement itself. Thus, the cigar stand sales at that time became a part of the sales figure on which operating cost ratios were based. In the restaurant statements examined in preparing this text, it was found to be general practice for restaurants to show the cigar stand profit under "Other Income", and that is the treatment now given to this phase of operation in the Uniform System of Accounts for Restaurants. Another point which is recognized in making this change is that by including the cigar stand profit as an item of "Other Income", the ratios of the restaurant expenses are based on their relation to food and beverage sales only, and the cigar stand operating result does not in any way affect these expense ratios.

CONTROLLABLE EXPENSES

The operating expenses, which are the direct responsibility of the management and are thus influenced by operating policies and efficiency, are listed under the major caption of "Controllable Expenses." These expenses are then divided into the groups or classes of expense under which they can best be summarized for the purpose of comparison. Thus, the controllable expenses are shown under the headings of Payroll, Employee Benefits, Employees' Meals, Direct Operating Expenses, Music and Entertainment, Advertising and Sales Promotion, Utilities, Administrative and General, and Repairs and Maintenance.

In general, all of the controllable expenses of a restaurant fall into one of these categories, and this major summary classification can be used for any restaurant, large or small. Most of the major categories can also be used to advantage by such feeding establishments as department stores, in-plant feeding, schools and colleges, hospitals, government and charitable institutions.

While the simplest form of statement will show this group of controllable expenses in one figure, the smaller operator should, in order to provide better control, divide these expenses into the major classifications shown in Exhibit A.

The salaries and wages paid are included under one major heading, "Payroll." This figure includes the service, preparation, and administrative payroll. In most restaurant statements this item is shown in one figure, but in some it is combined with social security taxes and other employee benefit costs to show a total "Labor Costs." In other statements examined, certain portions of the payroll are charged to administrative expense, utility costs, repairs and maintenance, etc. For the sake of uniformity, however, the cash payroll should be summarized under one heading and there should be proper sub-classifications as detailed as may seem desirable.

Since the beginning of the federal social security legislation and payroll taxes, it has been recognized that cash payroll is not the only labor cost in business and that there are now many other costs directly attributable to the restaurant staff and, to some extent, experienced in direct relation to it. These are such items as social security taxes, workmen's compensation insurance, group insurance, Blue Cross coverage and similar benefits. In addition, the restaurant may incur some further expense in providing for educational programs, group activities, functions, or other means of promoting employee good-will.

These expenses have now been covered in the Uniform System under one separate heading, "Employee Benefits" and this treatment is recommended in order that restaurants may achieve uniformity in their operating statements.

As previously mentioned, some statements reviewed show these expenses as a part of "Labor Cost" and others show them under "Administrative and General Expenses." However, when they are grouped under a separate heading coming directly after payroll, their effect on the operating result is apparent and at the same time the fact that the total is conveniently close to the payroll figure makes it possible to get a good idea of the total "Labor Cost."

The expenses incidental to service in the dining rooms, kitchen, storage and working spaces have been covered under one major heading, "Direct Operating Expenses." These expenses include such items as uniforms, laundry, cleaning and other supplies, menus, kitchen fuel, replacements of linens, china, glass, silver and utensils, etc.

The major change from the set-up recommended back in 1940 is the recognition that as a practical matter the replacements of linens, china, glassware, silver and utensils are regarded by the restaurant man as a constant expense, similar to the use of any of the other supplies needed in the conduct of his business. Therefore, it is advocated here that replacement costs of this type of equipment be included under this major heading as one of the "Direct Operating Expenses." In 1940 such replacements were included with the cost of repairs under the major heading of "Maintenance."

The item of music and entertainment cost is one that fluctuates sharply enough in the various types of restaurant operations to justify showing it separately in the Uniform System of Accounts for Restaurants. An ordinary street restaurant may not have any such expense or it may be nominal enough to warrant including it under "Miscellaneous Expenses" in the Direct Operating Expense group. On the other hand, as will be seen later in Exhibit E, the restaurant may depend on its music and entertainment program to develop business volume to a profitable point. This is particularly true in many specialty restaurants and night club type operations. In the latter instance, the music and entertainment costs will be a large factor in the expense of operation and will bring about a correspondingly marked change in its other expense ratios, particularly those of food, beverage and payroll costs.

Because this is an expense that is of prime importance to a relatively small group of restaurants, it has been shown under the Uniform System of Accounts For Restaurants in a separate figure and as a controllable expense. In this manner the idea of uniformity in statement presentation is fostered and the advantages of a comparison of the other cost and expense items is retained.

There is also a very wide fluctuation in advertising and promotion costs dependent on the policy of operation and, in many instances, on the type of patronage catered to. Thus, in the statements of some of the smaller restaurants there were few, if any, advertising and sales promotion expenditures. In the downtown restaurants, the expenditure was largely on newspaper and magazine advertising, while in the drive-in type establishment a considerable sum was spent on road signs. Direct mail, radio, and television advertising, and direct solicitation and other means were also used to promote sales.

For this reason, the expenditures for advertising and sales promotion were made a separate item on the summary profit and loss statement.

All utilities expense, except the cost of kitchen fuel, is included in a separate group. In many instances gas is used only for kitchen fuel and can easily be distributed as a direct operating expense. The same is true of charcoal and similar fuels. However, if electricity is used both as kitchen fuel and for light and power it becomes necessary to make a separation by means of a meter reading or an estimate, if the proprietor feels the item important enough to warrant accounting for it under the Uniform System.

In the 1940 Uniform System, heating and water costs were included under "Rent, Etc.," because in many rented establishments they were borne by the landlord and thus became a part of the rental cost. This is still true, but in the statements reviewed in preparing this text the restaurants who furnish their own heat and water usually grouped these costs with their other utility costs.

Therefore, as a practical matter and for the sake of uniformity, heat and water costs are included with the other utility costs in the Uniform System of Accounts for Restaurants. The thinking now is that the restaurant that furnishes its own heat and water is better informed about its operation if all utility costs are shown in one group, and the restaurant that has these utilities included in its rental should, therefore, keep this fact in mind when making comparisons of utility and rental costs with those of other restaurant operations.

Ice has also been included under utilities. Many restaurants now have their own ice machines, some of which are operated in connection with their refrigeration plants, and it would not be practical for them to isolate this cost. For the sake of uniformity, therefore, it is necessary for those who purchase ice from the outside to include it as a separate item of their utilities cost.

PROFIT BEFORE RENT OR OCCUPATION COSTS

The profit before rent or occupation costs and after deducting the controllable expenses is the point in the operating statement where restaurant management efficiency is judged. It is up to this point in the statement that the manager's efforts, combined with the operating policy or pattern of the restaurant, can to a great extent control the net profit result. Therefore, this figure is an important dividing line between management and ownership.

After this point in the statement the profit is dependent on the financial structure and the fixed obligations and expenses which have resulted from it.

Thus, it is highly important to arrive at the result at this stage before going on with any further study, as it is up to this point in the profit and loss statement that comparisons with other restaurant operations are practical and of real value.

PROFIT BEFORE DEPRECIATION

The profit before depreciation is another important division in the profit and loss statement, since it indicates the amount of cash funds that were made available for the principal payments on any mortgages, equipment contracts or loans; the payment of income taxes, and what is left for the proprietor after these obligations have been met. In some instances, the profit before depreciation is referred to as his "cash profit," although it must be remembered that the principal payments on his mortgages and loans, purchases of capital assets, and income taxes are still to come out of this figure.

DEPRECIATION

There is always considerable confusion in the minds of many restaurant men about depreciation. The building, furniture and equipment, leasehold and leasehold improvements, which represent a large part of the restaurant man's investment in the business, all have a limited useful life. They will ultimately be disposed of or be replaced because they have outlived their usefulness. This wearing out process is not something that can be seen or estimated from day to day; therefore, the cost is spread over the periods covered by the profit and loss statements prepared during their estimated useful life.

Thus, the costs charged against operations in the profit and loss statement represent the pro-rated amounts in recognition of the ultimate loss in value of the investment in these items. On the balance sheet the asset value is decreased by that same prorated amount to indicate its loss in value through use.

Because it is a proration of an expenditure already made and carried as an asset in the records, this prorated depreciation charge in the profit and loss statement does not require cash for its liquidation such as would be the case with other expenses.

It is for this reason that it is advocated in the profit and loss statement presentation that the profit be shown before depreciation and that the depreciation charge be deducted as a separate item.

INCOME TAXES

Many restaurants are operated by single proprietors or by partnerships, the owners of which have other interests or sources of income to account for in figuring their income taxes. For this reason their restaurant profit and loss statements will stop at the point of profit before income tax.

On the other hand, the federal and some state and city governments have declared themselves partners in the restaurant, as in other businesses, and income taxes are very much a part of the cost of doing business.

Many restaurants are operated by corporations, in which case the income tax becomes a part of its profit and loss statement.

EXHIBIT A

In a later section of this text there are illustrations of how the Uniform System of Accounts For Restaurants has been applied to the figures of several types of restaurant operations in the preparation of their Profit and Loss statements and balance sheets.

The following Exhibit A and its supporting schedules, together with the accompanying explanatory text, outlines the Uniform System of Accounts for Restaurants as approved by the Cost Study Committee of the National Restaurant Association.

SUMMARY PROFIT AND LOSS STATEMENT
NAME OF RESTAURANT OR COMPANY
DESCRIPTION OF PERIOD COVERED BY STATEMENT

	Schedule Number	Amounts	Percentages
SALES			
Food	A-1	$	%
Beverages	A-2		
Total food and beverage sales		$	100.00%
COST OF SALES			
Food			
Beverages			
Total cost of sales		$	%
GROSS PROFIT			
Food		$	%
Beverages			
Total gross profit		$	%
SERVICE CHARGES			
OTHER INCOME	A-3		
TOTAL INCOME		$	%
CONTROLLABLE EXPENSES			
Payroll	A-4	$	%
Service charge distribution			
Reserve for bonuses, vacation pay, etc.			
Employee benefits	A-5		
Employees' meals			
Direct operating expenses	A-6		
Music and entertainment	A-7		
Advertising and sales promotion	A-8		
Utilities	A-9		
Administrative and general expenses	A-10		
Repairs and maintenance	A-11		
Total controllable expenses		$	%
PROFIT BEFORE RENT OR OCCUPATION COSTS		$	%
RENT OR OCCUPATION COSTS	A-12		
PROFIT BEFORE DEPRECIATION		$	%
DEPRECIATION	A-12		
RESTAURANT PROFIT		$	%
ADDITIONS TO OR DEDUCTIONS FROM RESTAURANT PROFIT			
NET PROFIT BEFORE INCOME TAX		$	%
INCOME TAX			
NET PROFIT		$	%

FOOD SALES

	Meals Served	Amounts	Percentages
BY MEALS			
Breakfast		$	%
Lunch			
Dinner			
Supper			
		$	%
TOTAL DINING ROOMS			
Banquets and Parties			
TOTAL MEALS SERVED		$	%
BAKERY COUNTER			
TAKE-OUT SALES			
OUTSIDE CATERING			
TOTAL FOOD SALES		$	%

	Meals Served	Amounts	Percentages
BY DINING ROOMS			
Main Dining Room		$	%
Coffee Shop			
Counter or Lunch Room			
Grill			
Cafeteria			
Patio			
Drive-in			
Banquet Rooms			
TOTAL MEALS SERVED		$	%
BAKERY COUNTER			
TAKE-OUT SALES			
OUTSIDE CATERING			
TOTAL FOOD SALES		$	%

Food sales will include the sales of coffee, tea, milk and fruit juices, as these are usually served as part of a meal. If there is no service of liquor, beer or wines, the soft drink sales would also be included in this category. Sales taxes collected from the customer are not to be included in the total for food sales, but are intended to be credited to a separate liability account until such time as these taxes are paid to the government.

If pastry or baked goods are sold at a counter and the cost can be separated from that of the meals served patrons it may be desirable to show these sales and costs separately in the profit and loss statement. The same may be true of "take-out" sales of prepared foods, which, in some instances, have become a substantial source of income for the restaurant. If sufficiently large, these operations may require a separate departmental statement showing a departmental profit that would be included with "Other Income" as in the case of cigar stand sales which will be covered later in this section.

It may be very desirable to detail the make up of food sales in order to judge more accurately the kind of business being done. The most usual divisions are by types of meals or service and by dining rooms, as shown in Schedule A-1.

FOOD SALES STATISTICS

A knowledge of food sales statistics can be helpful in many ways. They might, for instance, indicate whether the menu setup is proper or the prices are right, whether management should concentrate on getting more customers or a higher average sale per meal, the efficiency of the layout as evidenced by sales per seat and the customer turnover per seat, and how efficiently the employees' time is scheduled as indicated by the number of meals served per waiter or waitress. For this reason, an example of such statistics and a description of how they are compiled is included here. This example is based on the figures in the daily report shown on Form No. 4 in Part III.

The sales are divided by the number of customers served and the resulting average check per customer is shown as follows:

Meal Period	Food Sales		Customers Served		Average Check
Breakfast.........................	$ 86.50	÷	144	=	$ .60
Lunch...........................	293.25	÷	245	=	1.20
Dinner	196.85	÷	81	=	2.43
Total	$576.60	÷	470	=	$1.23

If there were 100 seats in this restaurant the average daily sale and the daily customer turnover per seat would be as follows:

Meal Period	Daily Average Food Sales Per Seat	Daily Customer Turnover
Breakfast	$ .87	1.44
Lunch	2.93	2.45
Dinner	1.97	.81
Total	$5.77	4.70

At this restaurant five waitresses served breakfast, five served dinner, and the combined force served at the luncheon period. Thus, the customers and sales per waitress were calculated to be as follows:

Meal Period	Number of Waitresses	Average Sale Per Waitress	Customers Served Per Waitress
Breakfast	5	$17.30	28.8
Lunch	10	29.32	24.5
Dinner	5	39.37	16.2
Total	6.67	$86.49	70.5

(NOTE: 20 waitresses divided by the three meal periods equals 6.67 waitresses average for the day as shown on the total line).

21

It has been found practical to control payroll on the basis of production, as evidenced by the number of persons served in other positions such as cooks, dishwashers, etc., and some restaurants also maintain these payroll statistics.

Other statistics that are sometimes used for control purposes are the average number of pieces or pounds of laundry per cover, the number of cubic feet of gas, the kilowatt hours of electricity, etc.

However, in the ordinary restaurant the use of operating expense ratios and meal statistics should be sufficient amplification of the operating figures to give a restaurant man a clear picture of his business. He can always go into greater detail when something appears to be wrong, as indicated to him by the comparison of the regular statements from one period to the next.

If sales checks are used it is possible to analyze the food sales by items to determine just what has been sold. In so doing, the popularity of certain dishes may be determined, and the sales of such items as steaks and chops could be accounted for in the interests of providing closer control. An occasional test of checks in this manner might be quite revealing. Thus, it would be advisable to insist that guest checks, if used, be properly filled out by the waiter or waitress.

BEVERAGE SALES

	Amounts	Percentages
BY TYPES OF DRINKS		
Mixed Drinks and Cocktails	$	%
Beer and Ale		
Wines		
Soft Drinks		
Bottle Sales		
TOTAL BEVERAGE SALES	$	100.00%
BY BARS		
Main Bar	$	%
Service Bar		
Dining Room		
Grill		
Banquets and Parties		
Bottle Sales		
TOTAL BEVERAGE SALES	$	100.00%

The sales of beverages, which would include all alcoholic beverages and soft drinks, such as ginger ale, carbonated waters and set-ups, is shown separately on the profit and loss statement. As previously stated, these sales would not include coffee, tea, milk or fruit juices, which are considered food items inasmuch as they are normally served with meals. As stated in connection with food sales, the sales tax collected from the customer is not to be included in the beverage sales. However, if the sales tax is absorbed by the restaurant it may not be practical or advisable to separate these taxes for statement purposes and in such cases the tax on these sales becomes an administrative expense of operation, as explained later in this text.

Because the percentage of gross profit varies considerably for the different types of beverage sales, it may be helpful to operators to provide for a division of the beverage sales into several major groups such as sales of cocktails and liquors, wines, beers, non-alcoholic, and sales by the bottle, as shown in Schedule A-2. This might be done by means of separate keys on the bar cash register or by a daily analysis of the beverage checks.

Beverage sales might also be summarized by meal periods or by dining rooms and types of service.

It is not too practical to make a detailed analysis of sales for an open, or "cash" bar, but this can be done if all sales are recorded on guest checks and such an analysis may be important to cost control.

The number of customers served and the sales per customer are statistics that are more difficult to obtain on beverages than they are on food sales. For this reason, these statistics are not often recorded and they are also more difficult to interpret. The major point that is to be watched is the relation between food and beverage sales since their trends are normally similar, and any wide fluctuation in their relationship might indicate that something has gone wrong.

FOOD COST

The cost of food consumed is normally calculated in the following manner:

Beginning Inventory		$1,600.00
Add:		
Food Purchases	$6,750.00	
Express and Delivery Charges	55.00	6,805.00
Total		$8,405.00
Deduct:		
Ending Inventory		1,755.00
Cost of Food Consumed		$6,650.00

If a general storeroom is maintained the food purchases would be separated into food items such as milk, meats, etc., sent direct to the kitchen for production and the food items delivered to the storeroom and issued by requisition. In this case a separate control on the storeroom is desirable and the food cost calculation would probably be as follows:

STOREROOM

Beginning Inventory	$1,300.00
Food Stores Purchased	3,250.00
Total	$4,550.00
Issues per requisition	3,175.00
Balance to account for	$1,375.00
Ending inventory	1,325.00
Inventory over or (short)	(50.00)

The food issues from the storeroom plus or minus the inventory over or short would become a part of the cost of food consumed, calculated as follows:

Beginning kitchen inventory		$ 300.00
Direct food purchases	$3,500.00	
Storeroom (issues and shortage)	3,225.00	
Express and delivery	55.00	6,780.00
Total		$7,080.00
Ending kitchen inventory		430.00
Cost of food consumed ·		$6,650.00

The costs of coffee, tea, milk and soda fountain supplies are to be included in food cost. Where there is no service of alcoholic beverages the cost of drinks sold is also included in food cost.

EMPLOYEES' MEALS

The food cost calculations shown thus far do not take into consideration the amount of food used for employees' meals. Many of the smaller restaurants, and some of the larger ones, do not make any provision for the cost of employees' meals and thus their food costs are what are called "gross costs" or "cost of food consumed." It is for this reason that in the Uniform System the cost of employees' meals is shown as a separate item when it is calculated, and the profit and loss statement thus indicates that the food cost figure used in computing the gross profit is the net cost after deducting employees' meals.

Actually, the separation of the food cost between the cost of food served to guests and that served to employees is made in order to indicate more clearly the direct relation of menu prices to costs. At the same time, because meals served to employees are a part of their fringe benefits of employment and are included in figuring unemployment and retirement taxes, but not for withholding on Federal Income Tax, it is considered essential by many restaurant operators that such a calculation be made so that the amount can be watched and better controlled.

While there are many ways in which employees' meal costs are calculated, nearly all of them are based on food cost alone and no attempt is made to apportion payroll or other expenses of operation to this item. Of course, if a separate employees' dining room or cafeteria is maintained it may be possible to cost the food transfers to that room and charge the direct payroll and expenses of serving these meals. However, in most instances the employees use a part of the working or dining room space and serve themselves.

Thus, in the majority of cases, the policy of each individual restaurant with reference to meals allowed to employees is followed in arriving at a total count of meals from the payroll record. These meals are then priced on an estimated, and often arbitrary cost basis, and the number of meals times this cost per meal is the total cost of employees' meals.

Where certain employees, such as executives, department heads and others are served in the dining room, their meals are usually recorded on a special or "officers" check, at menu prices, and the amounts are not included with the sales to customers. In these instances the cost of employees' meals is calculated by the method shown in the following example:

Net Food Cost—Including Officers' Checks		Amount
Sales to customers		$20,000.00
Officers' checks		750.00
Total at menu prices		$20,750.00
Cost of food consumed		$ 8,637.50
Deduct: Cost of employees' meals not recorded on checks 1,350 meals at 25 cents		337.50
Net food cost—including officers' checks		$ 8,300.00
Ratio of Net Cost to Total at Menu Prices—$8,300.00 ÷ $20,750 =		40%

Employees' Meals Cost

Officers' checks $750.00 × 40%		$ 300.00
Meals not on checks		337.50
Total employees' meals		$ 637.50

Cost of Food Sold	Amount	Ratio to Sales
Sales to customers	$20,000.00	100.00%
Cost of food consumed	8,637.50	43.19%
Deduct: employees' meals	637.50	3.19%
Cost of Food Sold	$ 8,000.00	40.00%
Gross Profit on Food Sales	$12,000.00	60.00%

Whatever the method used, the amount calculated for employees' meals is influenced by the value placed on meals not recorded on checks. This amount can probably be estimated by someone familiar with the restaurant's policy with regard to the type of meals served to these employes. However, as stated before, in most instances the cost amount used per meal is arbitrarily chosen and, since many states and the federal social security regulations have indicated in past years that 25 cents per meal, or $4.50 per week, is acceptable, this is the usual amount used in calculating this cost. However, because of rising prices in the past few years, some states have increased this acceptable amount to 40 cents per meal, and it would be well to check with local regulations in making employees' meals calculations.

With the restaurant business coming under the jurisdiction of the Fair Labor Standards Act on February 1, 1967, the cost of employees' meals takes on a new aspect of importance. Under the Wage and Hour Law the employer is given a credit in determining the cash wage for the "Reasonable Cost" of board and lodging if either is customarily furnished to the employee. The regulations issued by the Wage and Hour Division state that the reasonable cost is "not more than the actual cost to the employer" of the meals furnished to employees. This cost cannot include any element of profit and is further defined as "the cost of operation and maintenance plus a reasonable allowance (not more than 5.5%) for interest on the depreciated amount of capital invested by the employer." These amounts must be determined under good accounting practices, and in no case can they exceed the fair price of the meals furnished.

We assume that this means that to the food commodity cost, which has up to now commonly been determined as outlined earlier in this section, must be added such costs as: help's hall, preparation, sanitation, purchasing and storeroom payroll, employee benefits as applied to such payroll, certain of the direct operating expenses as they may apply, utility costs, certain administrative expenses, repairs and maintenance, as they may apply. Up to 5.5% of the average equity capital invested can also be added proportionately to arrive at this "reasonable cost."

No set formula has as yet been outlined for determining this cost, and each restaurant involved must therefore determine the costs it will use subject to review by the Wage and Hour Division. We assume that most employers will tend to be conservative in determining this credit for the purpose of compliance with the Fair Labor Standards Act. Many restaurant operations, of course, already have cash wages in excess of the minimum hourly wage requirement and will not consider this a serious problem until the minimum wage reaches the higher levels set up in later years. However, they must keep in mind that this level rises from $1.00 in 1967 in 15 cent annual jumps to $1.60 in 1971, and that there is always the possibility that the law may be amended during this period. The meals credit, when determined, must be prorated on an hourly basis for the time of employment. Then, too, different amounts may represent the reasonable cost of different meals. For example, the reasonable hourly wage cost credit for breakfast might be 5 cents per hour, while the dinner credit could be 10 cents per hour. Another example of computation might be to multiply the hours worked by the minimum wage and to deduct the lump sum of reasonable cost of meals furnished. An illustration of this computation follows:

8 Hours worked at $1.00	$8.00
2 meals furnished at 50¢	1.00
Cash wage at 87.5¢ per hour	$7.00

There has been some confusion in the minds of restaurant operators regarding the treatment of employees' meal costs and this is bound to be accentuated by the requirements of the Wage and Hour Law. To clarify this matter we state the following rules applicable in accordance with past custom and present circumstances.

1. The cost of employees' meals as shown in the profit and loss statement of the restaurant is the commodity cost of food *only,* and it is offset as a credit to food cost, thus leaving a net cost of food served to guests or customers.

2. Often this employees' meal cost has been based on an arbitrary amount per meal rather than on an attempt to calculate the actual items served to employees. Some states have included these arbitrary amounts in their unemployment tax laws; for example, Illinois uses 25 cents per meal, Michigan and California use 40 cents per meal.

3. The Wage and Hour Law allows expenses in addition to food costs to be used as a credit in determining compliance with its minimum wage requirement. This amount is to be used for payroll purposes only and is not applicable to food cost. It would be impractical to apply this employees' wage credit to all of the expenses involved in the profit and loss statement, and this is not necessary for management control.

Thus, while many restaurant men have assumed that the employees' meal cost shown in the operating statements included payroll and other expenses in addition to food cost, it does so *only* on the payroll record indicating compliance with the laws relating to payroll. The food cost credit is applied on the payroll for the unemployment tax calculation and also in the profit and loss statement to determine the "Cost of Food Sold." The food cost before this credit is termed the "Cost of Food Consumed," which includes food served to employees.

4. Thus, it is possible to have three bases of cost for employees' meals.
   1. Food cost only—Profit and Loss Statement only to determine the net cost of food sold.
   2. Arbitrary credit—Payroll records only to determine social security and unemployment taxes.
   3. Reasonable cost—Payroll records only to determine compliance with the Fair Labor Standards Act.

The attempt is made in several states to assess a sales tax on employees' meals. This has been resisted by the various local restaurant associations on the basis that these meals are served as a part of the conditions of employment, and thus are an expense of operation and not a sale. In the federal income tax regulations, employees' meals are considered in this light and are not income to the recipient or a part of his wages for income tax purposes, provided that the meals are served on the restaurant premises and for the

27

convenience of the employer and not the employee. They are, however, for federal unemployment and retirement tax purposes considered as a part of wages paid.

Appendix A, following Part III of this text, contains suggestions on food control and food cost accounting.

BEVERAGE COST

The cost of beverages is ordinarily computed as follows:

Beginning inventory		$2,000.00
Add:		
Purchases	$2,100.00	
Bar groceries		
(Transferred from Food Cost)	100.00	
Express and Delivery charges	60.00	2,260.00
Total		$4,260.00
Deduct ending inventory		1,850.00
Cost of beverages		$2,410.00

If a storeroom or wine room is maintained it would be advisable to control it by means of a perpetual inventory. All purchases of liquors, wines, beers and waters would be charged to the wine room and issued on requisition as they are needed at the bar. It is also advisable to establish a par stock for the bar, which is to be maintained by replenishing the stock each morning. In this manner the morning requisition, plus the interim issues to the bar the day before, will approximate the beverage cost for that day which can be compared with the sales for daily control purposes.

In this case a separate control is kept on the wine room stock and the beverage cost would be figured as follows:

WINE ROOM

Beginning inventory	$1,500.00
Purchases	2,100.00
Total	$3,600.00
Issues to bar	2,240.00
Balance	$1,360.00
Ending inventory	1,365.00
Inventory over or (short)	$ 5.00

Thus, the issues to the bar plus the wine room shortage, or minus the wine room overage, would become a part of the cost of beverages calculated as follows:

Beginning Bar Stock		$ 500.00
Add:		
Wine room (issues less overage)	$2,235.00	
Bar groceries	100.00	
Express and cartage	60.00	2,395.00
Total		$2,895.00
Deduct ending bar stock		485.00
Cost of beverages		$2,410.00

The bar inventory should certainly be taken at least once a month and, in many instances, it is taken once a week. It will, of course, fluctuate depending on how accurately it is replenished from the wine room stock each day and how accurately it is taken, for there will always be partially filled bottles to be considered. It has been advocated that part bottles be calculated to the 10th of a bottle as a practical matter in taking and pricing this bar inventory. Thus, even if a par stock is maintained, the inventory values will fluctuate slightly because of the partially filled bottles, changes in cost prices, and the shortages and overages in the inventory count. These fluctuations in bar inventory will add or subtract from the beverage cost. For instance, in the calculations used as an illustration the wine room inventory showed an overage of $5.00 and the bar inventory went down $15.00.

As stated under "Food Cost" the costs of coffee, tea, milk and soda fountain supplies are to be included in food cost. Where there is no service of alcoholic beverages the cost of soft drinks is also included in food cost.

SERVICE CHARGES

Some hotels, motels and restaurants, particularly in resort areas, are adopting the policy of adding service charges to the customers' checks as a means of eliminating the necessity of keeping records on the tips received by tipped employees. Several restaurants had already adopted this policy as a public relations measure before they came under the Wage and Hour Act. However, public acceptance has been a controversial issue which deters the majority of restaurants from following the policy of adding service charges to the menu prices.

Some restaurants distribute the entire service charge income to service employees, some distribute a portion to certain other employees as well and some distribute only a portion, retaining a small percentage to cover book-keeping costs, etc., or to be distributed later as bonuses. Some other restaurants have increased their payroll rates to compensate service help for the amounts considered in lieu of tips.

In order not to disturb the payroll percentage relation of costs to food and beverage sales, which sales are still the primary and basic items of restaurant income, the Uniform System of Accounts for Restaurants urges that this service charge income be shown as a separate amount or item in the profit and loss statement, to be added to gross profit together with "other income" in arriving at total income. In this way the restaurants that follow the "service charge" policy are still in a position to compare results with those that do not.

Likewise, as outlined later under the Expense Section of the Profit and Loss Statement, the Service Charge Distribution and Reserve for Bonuses is to be shown as a separate amount directly following the item of payroll. In this manner the service charge distribution will not be as confusing an item in making payroll comparisons with other restaurant operations. As a further advantage, the total effect of resorting to a "service charge" policy will be plainly outlined in the profit and loss statement.

The question arises as to whether such service charges are to be considered a part of sales for state and local tax purposes. It appears logical that, since the service charge is made in lieu of tips to the employee, it is a part of the payroll cost paid by the customer and not a part of the retail sales. This is plainly outlined by the treatment of this item under the Uniform System, which includes such income after determining gross profit on food and beverage sales.

Of course, any service charge income not distributed to employees becomes a part of net income, as it is not practical to deduct the Bookkeeping Charges, etc. from General and Administrative Expense.

OTHER INCOME

	Amounts
Cover Charges and Minimum Charges	$
Banquet Room Rentals	
Cigar Stand	
Rental on Shops, Display Cases, etc.	
Concession Rentals—Coat Room, Washroom, Parking	
Vending Machine Commissions—Cigarettes, Candy, Sanitary Items, Music Machines	
Telephone and Coin Box Commissions	
Salvage and Waste Sales	
Cash Discounts	
Other Miscellaneous Items, such as Menu Advertising, etc.	
TOTAL OTHER INCOME	$

Under this heading the Uniform System of Accounts for Restaurants includes all of the restaurant operating income other than food and beverage sales, as indicated in Schedule A-3.

In most instances it would be advisable to show the details on how the cigar stand gross profit is arrived at by means of a separate schedule or statement, illustrated as follows:

CIGAR STAND OPERATION	Amount	Ratios to Sales
Sales		
Tobacco—Cigars	$ 200.00	13.33%
Cigarettes	800.00	53.34
Candy and Gum	150.00	10.00
Novelties	350.00	23.33
Total Sales	$1,500.00	100.00%
Cost of Sales		
Tobacco—Cigars	$ 160.00	80.00%
Cigarettes	720.00	90.00
Candy and Gum	112.50	75.00
Novelties	227.50	65.00
Total Cost of Sales	$1,220.00	81.33%
Gross Profit—To Other Income	$ 280.00	18.67%

In some instances the cost of book matches used by the cigar stand is also charged to its cost although, in many instances, this item is considered a direct operating expense and classified under "Guest Supplies", or, if used outside the restaurant as an advertising medium, they are charged to advertising and promotion expense.

In large operations grease sales are sometimes credited to food cost, but in the small restaurant it is practical to include sales of waste paper, bottles and grease under "Other Income." Lately, in many areas this problem is obviated by the fact that the restaurant operator must now pay for removal of all garbage and waste matter; thus, it becomes an expense rather than an income item.

Cash discounts, if they are recorded, may be included in this income group; but in most small restaurants it is more practical to consider these discounts as a reduction of the cost of the item purchased and to enter only the net amount paid on the invoice in the cash disbursements sheet.

It is important to point out that only income resulting from, or associated directly with, the operation of the restaurant should be included in this income group. Any income from rentals, interest, dividends, etc., received on other investments of the restaurant company are to be shown at the bottom of the profit and loss statement just ahead of the income tax provision, under the heading "Additions to Income" which will be commented on later in this section.

PAYROLL

	Number of Employees	Amounts	
		Regular Payroll	Extra Wages
SERVICE			
Headwaiter, Headwaitress, Chief Hostess		$	$
Captains, Hostesses, Receptionists			
Waiters, Waitresses, Car-hops			
Counter Service (Cafeteria)			
Bus Boys, Bus Girls, Runners, Pages			
Banquet or Extra Waiters, Waitresses			
Cashiers and Checkers			
Order Clerks (Bakery or Take-out Counter)			
Total Service		$	$
BEVERAGES			
Wine Steward and Wine Room Attendants		$	$
Bartenders			
Bar Porters			
Beverage Controller and Bar Cashiers			
Total Beverages		$	$
PREPARATION			
Chef, Head Dietitian, Kitchen Manager		$	$
Cooks, Cold Meats, Oysterman			
Short Order Cooks			
Fountain Attendants			
Pantry and Salads			
Butcher Shop, Bake Shop, Pastry and Ice Cream			
Coffee Attendant			
Potwashers			
Vegetable Cleaners			
Iceman			
Runners			
Steward and Assistants			
Total Preparation		$	$
SANITATION			
Dishwashers, Glasswashers, Silvermen		$	$
Porters			
Night Cleaners			
Garbage Man			
Total Sanitation		$	$
PURCHASING AND STORING			
Purchasing Steward		$	$
Receiving Clerk			
Storeroom Men			
Food Controller			
TOTAL PAYROLL (CARRIED FORWARD)		$	$

33

PAYROLL

	Number of Employees	Amounts	
		Regular Payroll	Extra Wages
TOTAL PAYROLL (Brought Forward)		$	$
ADMINISTRATIVE			
Administrative and Officers' Salaries		$	$
Manager			
Manager's Office			
Banquet Sales Office (Outside Catering, etc.)			
Accounting Office			
Personnel and Payroll Office			
Data Processing Payroll			
Telephone Operators			
Watchmen			
Total Administrative		$	$
OTHER			
Engineers		$	$
Maintenance Men			
Gardeners			
Doormen			
Cloak Room and Washroom Attendants			
Parking Lot Attendants			
Cigar Stand Clerks			
Total Other		$	$
TOTAL PAYROLL		$	$

As previously stated, under the Uniform System of Accounts For Restaurants the entire payroll is included under one major group, since that is the way it is shown in the large majority of restaurant profit and loss statements. This amount includes the regular salaries and wages, extra wages, overtime, vacation pay, and any commission or bonus payments made to employees.

In some large restaurants and chain organizations the payroll of the central commissary, bake shop, or administrative office is included in the statements of these particular departments, and then it is apportioned to the restaurant profit and loss statement in accordance with a formula derived by the individual operation.

Also, in the case of single proprietors and partnerships, the payment to the owners in recognition of their management efforts is represented in the net profit or in their cash drawings from the business and does not appear as part of the payroll; whereas, in restaurants operating under what is known as a "closed-corporation" the administrative payroll might include officers' salaries that could, under other circumstances, be deemed disproportionately high. Although it might, under either circumstance, be feasible and practical in individual instances to arrive at a management and administrative salary that would be comparable to that paid a hired manager performing the same services, in general a change in payroll setup is inadvisable. It is well, however, to keep this matter of proprietors' or partners' salaries in mind when making comparisons of the individual restaurant with others under the Uniform System.

If it seems desirable, a sub-classification can be made of the payroll by dividing it into such major groups as service, preparation, warewashing, storeroom, clerical and administrative. It might also be desirable to further divide the payroll according to the various dining areas served, such as main dining room, coffee shop, cafeteria, cocktail lounge and bar, banquets and parties, etc.

Schedule A-4 illustrates a suggested detailed payroll distribution indicating the number of employees in the regular payroll, their regular pay, and the amount of extra wages. Another example of how one large restaurant details its payrolls in the monthly profit and loss statement is shown in Part II of this book, Schedule G-1.

The item of "vacation pay" has been of some concern, and many restaurant operators keep a separate account of it. Although vacation pay is actually one of the employees' benefits, it is not shown in Schedule A-5 which follows, as it is more practical to include this cost with the cash payroll, shown separately in the proper category in the payroll schedule, when the calculation is made.

SERVICE CHARGE DISTRIBUTION

Where service charges are made in lieu of tips, the distribution to employees is actually the payroll cost portion borne directly by the customer. For this reason the amount of these distributions is shown as a separate item in the Profit and Loss Statement immediately following the item of "Payroll." By so doing, the entire payroll cost is obtainable in one section of the profit and loss statement, and yet the comparison of payroll costs with restaurants not making service charges is more significant.

RESERVE FOR BONUSES, VACATION PAY, ETC.

If a bonus portion of service charges is retained for later distribution, the amount so reserved should also be shown as a separate item immediately following "Service Charge Distributions" and the amount will be credited to a reserve shown in the Current Liability section of the Balance Sheet, which reserve will be closed out when the bonuses are paid.

Some restaurant operators spread the cost of vacations by setting up a reserve for vacation pay during the year and charging the reserve when the vacations are actually taken and paid for. If this policy is followed it is recommended that the same statement treatment be used as that recommended for the bonus reserve.

EMPLOYEE BENEFITS

	Amounts
SOCIAL SECURITY TAXES	
Federal Insurance Contributions (Retirement Tax)	$
Federal Unemployment Tax	
State Unemployment Tax	
State Health Insurance Tax	
Total Payroll Taxes	$
SOCIAL INSURANCE	
Workmen's Compensation Insurance Premiums	$
Welfare Plan Payments	
Pension Plan Payments	
Accident and Health Insurance Premiums	
Hospitalization, Blue Cross, Blue Shield, etc.	
Group Insurance Premiums	
Total Social Insurance	$
OTHER EXPENSES	
Employee Instruction and Education Expense	$
Employee Christmas and Other Parties	
Employee Sports Activities	
Medical Expenses	
Credit Union	
Awards and Prizes	
Transportation and Housing (Roadside and Resort Areas)	
Total Other Expenses	$
TOTAL EMPLOYEE BENEFITS	$

The accounts to be included in this group are detailed in Schedule A-5.

EMPLOYEES' MEALS

The calculation and treatment of employees' meals in the Profit and Loss Statement under the Uniform System of Accounts for Restaurants has been described in detail earlier in this text in connection with food cost.

Although employees' meals might properly be considered as an item of employees' benefits expense, it seems more practical, in the interest of gaining uniformity in statement presentation, to show this item separately in the summary statement of profit and loss. This method makes it possible to show not only the amount of this expense and its relation to the other major elements of operation, but also, by its presence in the statement, to indicate that the food cost figure shown is after the deduction of employees' meals.

Many of the smaller restaurant operators, and some of the larger ones, make no calculation of the cost of employees' meals; in these cases, the gross food cost or "Cost of Food Consumed" is shown in the Profit and Loss Statement. With the restaurant business now coming under the jurisdiction of the

Wage and Hour Division of the Federal Labor Department, it is anticipated that more restaurant operators will give consideration to calculating the cost of employees' meals as outlined in the Food Cost section of this text.

Spurred by the requirements under the Fair Labor Standards Act, some hotel and restaurant operators are considering adopting the policy of charging employees for their meals (at discount prices) and increasing their cash wages accordingly. This policy obviates the necessity of calculating "Reasonable Cost" and of considering menu restrictions to employees. It is also considered by some operators as providing a tighter control, which results in savings on employees' meal cost. This again brings up the possible question of sales taxes on meals served to employees under this policy.

DIRECT OPERATING EXPENSES

	Amounts
	$
Uniforms	
Laundry	
Linen Rental	
Linens	$
China and Glassware	
Silverware	
Kitchen Utensils	_____
Kitchen Fuel	
Cleaning Supplies	$
Paper Supplies	
Guest Supplies	
Bar Supplies	_____
Menus and Drink Lists	
Dry Cleaning	
Contract Cleaning	
Flowers and Decorations	
Auto or Truck Expense	
Employee Transportation	
Freight, Express and Cartage	
Parking	
Licenses and Permits	
Banquet Expense	
Miscellaneous	_____
TOTAL DIRECT OPERATING EXPENSES	$

The various items that are indicated under this major heading demand more than a mere listing to describe them properly and give the reasons for their inclusion. For the most part, they are expenses directly involved in the service to the customer, which is why they are described as "Direct Expenses." An attempt is made, insofar as possible, to list the closely related expenses next to each other, so that they might be combined in the profit and loss statement if the restaurant operator does not want as extensive a listing of accounts as is shown in Schedule A-6. At the same time, it should be noted from some of the descriptions that it is possible to divide the items into even greater detail than is shown by the accounts listed.

UNIFORMS

This amount includes the cost of all uniforms purchased, the cost of cleaning and repairing them and the cost of badges. Some of the items included under uniform expense are:

Aprons	Ties
Blouses	Trousers
Caps	Shirtfronts
Coats	Hairnets
Collars	Shoes
Dresses	Bonnets
Smocks	Costumes
Gloves	Badges
Suits	

LAUNDRY

This category includes the cost of laundering table linens and uniforms, napkins, towel and apron service.

LINEN RENTAL

If the linen is not owned by the restaurant but is rented, such rental service cost is shown in this account, or it may, for convenience, be included with the laundry cost, as linen and laundry services are often related and supplied by the same company.

REPLACEMENT OF LINEN, CHINA, GLASSWARE, SILVER, UTENSILS

It was established by the reference to their operating statements that restaurant men consider the replacement cost of linens, china, glassware, silver and utensils as a direct service cost rather than as a repair and maintenance item, and for this reason the Uniform System of Accounts For Restaurants includes these replacements in the direct operating expense group. This is the same as the treatment given these items in the Uniform System of Accounts for Hotels and Clubs.

As was pointed out in the introductory letter, this is a change in the classification of these operating equipment items from the major grouping recommended back in 1942, at which time these items were considered a part of maintenance expenses.

In the small restaurant the cost of these replacements is usually charged to expense when the purchase is recorded and very often all of these costs are grouped into one account. However, since these replacement purchases are often made in quantities that would distort the expense ratios in the month in which they are purchased, a more equitable method would be to make monthly charges equal to a pro-rata share of maintaining this equipment at a practical level, by basing the charges on a ratio to food and beverage sales which has been indicated by past experience or by comparison with the averages for other restaurants. The amount of these estimated charges to expense is credited to a reserve account, and the cost of the actual replacements is charged against this reserve. At the close of the year this reserve can be adjusted to equal the purchases for that year, if no inventories are taken of this equipment, or to the amounts actually used up if the equipment is controlled by means of inventories.

The most accurate accounting for these items is based on adjustments to actual inventories taken at stated periods and priced at fair values in accordance with the age and condition of the equipment.

In valuing these inventories, it is practical to use the last purchase price for each item as a base. Because linens, china and silverware are in constant use and replaced as they wear out, it can be assumed for all practical purposes that the average equipment in use has already experienced half of its useful life and thus could be valued at one-half its cost price in the inventory. This is not true with glassware, which is either worth 100% or, if chipped or cracked, should be discarded.

Kitchen and bar utensils are seldom accounted for by inventory since there are so many items included that the detail and time involved is not considered worth while and thus these items are, for the most part, charged to expense as purchased.

Any reserve stock of operating equipment in storage or in unopened packages should be valued at 100% of cost.

The transactions for the year in these operating equipment accounts are illustrated by the following example of a typical silver equipment account.

INVENTORY ACCOUNT

Beginning Silver Inventory		
In use —at 50% value	$12,000.00	
In Reserve—at 100% value	1,550.00	$13,550.00
Adjustments to close out reserve balance (see below)		400.00
Net Balance		$13,150.00
Adjustment to operating expense (direct operating expenses—silver)		
To reflect decrease in ending inventory		50.00
Ending silver inventory		
In Use —at 50% value	$11,500.00	
In Reserve—at 100% value	1,600.00	
Total Ending Inventory..		$13,100.00

RESERVE ACCOUNT

Monthly Credits To Reserve	
For charges to Direct Operating Expenses—Silver	$ 1,200.00
Purchases Charged to Reserve	800.00
Reserve Balance closed out to Inventory Account (see above)	400.00

DIRECT OPERATING EXPENSE ACCOUNT—SILVER

Monthly Charges Credited to Reserve	$ 1,200.00
Adjustment to Ending Inventory Values (see above)	50.00
Total Expense for the Year..	$ 1,250.00

This illustration demonstrates that through the use of inventories on this equipment, it is possible to determine the actual cost of its use, which is a more accurate amount than if the $800.00 of replacement purchases for the year were accepted as the cost to be charged to expense.

As a practical matter, particularly in the smaller restaurant, inventories are not usually taken on this type of equipment and thus these expenses are based on the actual purchases, and the inventories' fluctuations are disregarded. These inventory methods are mentioned for the benefit of those who desire a more accurate statement of these costs.

LINENS

Linens are placed first in this operating equipment group on the statement because of their relationship to laundering and linen rental costs.

Items included in this group are:

Napkins	Table Tops
Table Cloths	Table Protectors
Doilies	Side Towels

CHINA AND GLASSWARE

The costs for replacement of these items are usually accounted for together, although, in some instances, the beverage glassware replacements are shown separately on the profit and loss statement.

Items included in this group are:

Plates	Pitchers
Cups	Drinking Glasses
Saucers	Goblets
Bowls	Wine Glasses
Compotes	Shot Glasses
Coffee and tea pots	Tumblers
Platters	Cordial Glasses
Trays	

SILVERWARE

In addition to the cost of replacement of these items this account will be charged with the cost of re-plating and repairing silverware.

The items in this group include:

Flatware	Ice Cream Dishes
Hollow Ware	Bowls
Ladles	Platters
Serving Dishes	Trays
Candelabra and	
Decorative pieces	

UTENSILS

This account includes the cost of replacing tools and small equipment used in the kitchen and the cost of their repair, including knife sharpening, soldering, etc.

The items in this group are:

Knives	Mixing Bowls
Cleavers and other tools	Beaters
Pots	Skewers
Pans	Mixing Spoons
Kettles	Can Openers

Bar utensils are not included here as they are listed as a bar expense.

KITCHEN FUEL

Fuel used for cooking to be charged to this account includes:

Gas	Prepared Heat Substances
Coal	Steam
Charcoal	Electricity
Brickettes	Hickory Chips

If electric ranges and ovens are used, the current should be metered separately from that used for light and power. The same is true of live steam for cooking. Where the use of electricity for cooking is incidental, it is not practical to determine the cost and any effort to do so is unwarranted.

SUPPLIES USED

In the case of the smaller restaurant this group of expenses may be put in one account; in the larger operations, however, they should be divided into cleaning supplies, paper supplies, guest supplies, and bar supplies.

CLEANING SUPPLIES

Items to be included here are suggested by the following:

Cleaning Fluids	Brooms and Sweepers
Cleaning Compounds	Mops
Polish	Brushes
Soaps	Cleaning Cloths
Detergents	Dust Cloths
Disinfectants	Pails
Cleaning Chemicals	Rags
(BB) Shot	Steel Wool
Deodorants	

PAPER SUPPLIES

Chop Frills	Sippers
Cups	Souffle Cups
Doilies	Ramekins
Liners	Holders
Napkins	Pastry Bags
Plates	Filter Paper
Wrapping Paper	Wax Paper
Boxes	Twine

GUEST SUPPLIES

This account should include the cost of all items furnished to dining room patrons, such as:

Matches	Tooth Picks
Favors and small gifts	Score pads for cards
Newspapers	Prizes
Souvenirs	Postal Cards

BAR SUPPLIES

This account will include the cost of bar utensils and other supplies such as:

Corkscrews	Measuring Rules
Mixers	Knives
Bottle Openers	Strainers
Shakers	Bottle Stoppers
Spoons	Swizzle Sticks
Fruit Squeezers	Toothpicks
Fancy Drink Decorations	Gratis food
Favors and small gifts	*(not used in mixed drinks such*
Souvenirs	*as nuts, popcorn, etc.)*

MENUS AND DRINK LISTS

The cost of art work, cuts, paper stock and printing of menus, bills-of-fare and beverage lists, whether they are purchased from the outside or prepared by the restaurant's own facilities, should be included in this category. Where the cost is too small to warrant separation this expense might be combined with printing and stationery expense, under the general heading of "Administrative and General Expenses", detailed in a later paragraph.

DRY CLEANING

This account should be charged with the cost of dry cleaning curtains, draperies, hangings, etc., the cost of washing or cleaning awnings, carpets, rugs, window shades, and chair coverings.

CONTRACT CLEANING

The cost of service contracts for night cleaning, window washing, extermination and disinfecting service should be charged to this account.

In many of the restaurant statements reviewed in preparing this text, the items included under this heading are shown separately on the profit and loss statement.

FLOWERS AND DECORATIONS

Items to be included in this account are the cost of cut flowers, ferns, palms, artificial flowers, ribbons, flags, bunting, decorative pieces prepared for tables or display, song birds, goldfish, etc., used for table or dining room decoration. It will also include the cost of the services of any florist, window dresser or similar specialists. The cost of special holiday decorations would also be charged to this account. Ice carvings used as table decorations or display should also be charged here.

If special decorations or flowers are purchased for banquets and parties and the customer is charged for them separately from the cost of the meal, this cost should be offset against the income which would be shown under "Other Income."

AUTO OR TRUCK EXPENSE

Some restaurants maintain their own automobile or truck for the transportation of food and supplies from the market, or for delivery purposes in the case of outside catering. This is particularly true of drive-in type operations which are located outside the center of town. This account should be charged with the cost of gasoline, oil, licenses, repairs, etc., in connection with these cars used in the business. If a car rental or delivery service contract is used, the cost should also be included here.

EMPLOYEE TRANSPORTATION

In the case of restaurant operations located away from the center of town, it is often necessary to provide employees with transportation to and from work or to furnish bus fare or travel allowance for this purpose. Where a company bus or automobile is used this transportation cost will be included in "Auto or Truck Expense."

FREIGHT, EXPRESS AND CARTAGE

Although it is advisable to charge freight, express and cartage costs in connection with food and beverage purchases to the food and beverage cost, these expenses are often shown in the expense section of the profit and loss statement. Therefore, if this is found to be a more practical procedure, these expenses should be included in this direct operating expense category.

PARKING

Parking of customers' automobiles has become a major problem in many restaurant operations. Any parking lot rental, garage, or other costs in connection with the parking of customers' cars should be included in this account.

LICENSES AND PERMITS

This account should be charged with all federal, state, and municipal licenses in connection with the restaurant, bar, food, or cabaret operations. The cost of special permits and inspection fees should also be included here.

No sales, franchise, or other taxes, however, are to be charged to this account as they are provided for elsewhere in the profit and loss statement.

BANQUET EXPENSE

Included in this account are expenses incurred in connection with banquet and party service which cannot properly be included in other expense groups already listed. Such items would be chair or equipment rental, party favors, special decorations, etc.

MISCELLANEOUS

This classification is to include all items attributable directly to the service of the customer that cannot be classified under previous headings, such as the cost of laboratory tests, special officers, lost and damaged articles, snow shoveling, etc.

MUSIC AND ENTERTAINMENT

Amounts

Orchestras and Musicians $
Professional Entertainers
Mechanical Music
Muzack or Other Wire Services
Piano Rental and Tuning
Films, Records, Sheet Music
Programs
Royalties to ASCAP, BMI and SESAC
Booking Agent's Fees
Meals Served to Musicians and Entertainers   _____

TOTAL MUSIC AND ENTERTAINMENT $

NOTE: The items of this schedule are self-explanatory and fully descriptive of the costs and expenses to be charged to this account and they are not, therefore, discussed in further detail.

ADVERTISING AND SALES PROMOTION

Amounts

Newspaper Advertising $
Magazines and Trade Journal Advertising
Circulars, Brochures, Postal Cards and Other Mailing Pieces
Direct Mail
Postage used for Advertising and Promotion
Telephone and Telegraph used for Advertising and Promotion
Sales Representative Service
Advertising or Promotional Agency Fees
Travel Expense on Solicitation
Outdoor Signs and Road Signs
Broadcasting, Radio and Television
Civic and Community Projects
Donations
Programs, Directories and Guides
Souvenirs, Favors, Treasure Chest Items
Entertaining Costs in Promotion of Business
    (Including Gratis Meals, etc., to Customers)
Preparation of Copy, Photographs, etc.   _____

TOTAL ADVERTISING AND SALES PROMOTION $

This account will be charged with all costs incurred in the maintenance, creation, or promotion of sales in the restaurant as indicated in Schedule A-8.

The reason donations are included here is that they are usually given to secure and maintain good-will of the community toward the restaurant.

Help-Wanted advertising is not charged here, but as an administrative and general expense.

44

UTILITIES

	Amounts
Electricity	$
Electric Bulbs	
Fuel	
Water	
Ice and Refrigeration Supplies	
Removal of Waste	
Engineer's Supplies	————
TOTAL UTILITIES	$
Deduct Credits	
Sales to Tenants — Electricity $	
Water, etc. ————	————
NET UTILITY COST TO RESTAURANT	$

This group of expenses, although direct in nature in that they contribute to the comfort of and service to the customer, lends itself to a natural major grouping and includes the following listed items:

ELECTRICITY

The cost of electricity purchased is charged to this account. Where current is metered separately for light and power it may be desirable to show the cost of each

Where all or a major part of the cooking or baking is done by electricity, the current should be metered separately or the amount used otherwise determined and it should be charged to direct operating expenses as "Kitchen Fuel."

ELECTRIC BULBS

This account is self-explanatory.

FUEL

This account should include the cost of all fuel except that charged to direct operating expenses under the caption "Kitchen Fuel." The type of fuel used should be stated, such as coal, oil, gas or steam.

In some instances where the restaurant is in rented property, the rental charge might include heat and possibly also water costs. As was stated in the introductory section of this book, back in 1940 this situation was recognized and handled by including heat and water costs in the rent or occupation cost section of the profit and loss statement. However, in a review of many operating statements, it was found that restaurants which pay for their own heat and water group these costs with the other utility costs of the restaurant. Therefore, as a practical matter and for the sake of uniformity, these costs have been included under this major heading, which puts all utility costs together.

45

WATER

This account is charged with the cost of water consumed and with any chemicals, such as water softener or purifying compounds used.

ICE AND REFRIGERATION SUPPLIES

Where no general refrigeration plant or ice machines are used and ice is purchased from outside concerns, the cost, including that of dry ice, should be charged to this account.

The cost of supplies for the refrigeration plant, including ammonia, brine, calcium and other refrigerants, should also be charged here.

Ice purchased to be used for ice carvings as table or banquet decorations should, of course, be charged to direct operating expenses under the caption "Flowers and Decorations."

The restaurant man may feel that ice used for table and bar service should also be considered a direct operating expense rather than a utility cost. However, since the advent of the ice-cube machine conveniently located for restaurant and bar service, the nature of this expense has changed and in a uniform statement presentation it is more logical to charge all refrigeration and ice production costs and ice purchases in one account as a utility item.

REMOVAL OF WASTE

This account will be charged with the cost of garbage disposal and of the removal of rubbish and waste matter, usually done under contract. Any incinerator expense would also be included here.

Years back restaurants obtained an income from the sale of garbage, paper, bottles, etc., but in the last few years disposing of them has become an expense item.

ENGINEER'S SUPPLIES

The cost of oils, boiler compound, fuses, grease, solvents, packing and other supplies plus any small tools used in the operation or maintenance of the mechanical and electrical equipment should be charged to this account.

CREDITS TO UTILITY COSTS

In the event that the restaurant has income from the sale of electric current, ice, steam, water or other utility items to a tenant, sub-tenant or concessionaire, these sales should be regarded as a reduction in the utility costs of the restaurant and should be credited to this group of expenses.

ADMINISTRATIVE AND GENERAL EXPENSES

	Amounts
Office Stationery, Printing and Supplies	$
Postage	
Telephone and Telegraph	
Management Fees	
Executive Office Expenses	
Data Processing Costs	
Directors' or Trustees' Fees	
Dues and Subscriptions	
Traveling Expenses	
Insurance — General	
Fee to Credit Organizations	
Collection Fees	
Provision for Doubtful Accounts	
Cash Shortages	
Claims and Damages Paid	
Professional Fees	
Protective Services	
Bank Deposit Pick-up Services	
Royalties	
Franchise Fees	
Sales Taxes	
Personnel Expense, Help Wanted Ads, etc.	
Miscellaneous	
TOTAL ADMINISTRATIVE AND GENERAL EXPENSES	$

This group of expenses is commonly considered as "overhead," and the items included here are those necessary to the operation of the business rather than those connected directly with the service and comfort of the customer.

OFFICE STATIONERY, PRINTING AND SUPPLIES

This account should be charged with the cost of all printed matter not devoted to advertising and promotion, such as accounting forms, account books, restaurant checks, office supplies, cash register and other checking supplies, letterheads, bills and envelopes.

POSTAGE

All postage except amounts applicable to advertising should be charged here.

TELEPHONE AND TELEGRAPH

The cost of telephone equipment rental, local and long distance calls, and telegrams, should be charged to this account with the exception of calls chargeable to advertising and promotion.

In instances where an inter-communication system such as Telautograph, pneumatic tube or teletype is in use, the cost of service and supplies used in connection with it may also be charged to this account.

47

MANAGEMENT FEES

Fees charged by a management organization or by the central office of a chain operation for executive supervision and management should be charged to this account.

In cases where the manager's compensation is on the basis of a salary plus a percentage of profit, it might also be of interest to show the amount of percentage participation as a separate item in the profit and loss statement.

DATA PROCESSING COSTS

With the development of electronic data processing machines and computers adaptable to the record keeping of smaller business organizations, many restaurants are using data processing in preparing their payrolls, for control of restaurant checks and to obtain detail helpful to management on sales and costs, which was heretofore too time consuming to be done by hand posting. Some have even programmed their entire records and statements for data processing. As this type of equipment becomes more adaptable and less costly, it is anticipated that more and more restaurants will turn to data processing for the advantages in control and additional helpful detail it can provide. The data processing equipment rental or fees to banks and other organizations providing this service should be entered under this heading.

Up to the present time this service would not result in payroll savings for office help in the normal restaurant organization except, perhaps, for payroll records. However, the additional detail available to management may make this type of expenditure worthwhile.

EXECUTIVE OFFICE EXPENSES

The proportionate share of central office expenses charged to the restaurant by a chain operation should be charged to this account, as should any traveling or other expenses incurred by the executives of the central office in connection with supervisory visits.

DIRECTORS' AND TRUSTEES' FEES

The fees and expenses of directors, trustees, registrars or others in like capacity should be charged to this account.

DUES AND SUBSCRIPTIONS

The dues paid for the restaurant's membership in trade or business organizations or for authorized members of the staff to represent the restaurant in such associations are charged to this account. The cost of subscriptions to trade papers and magazines used by the management or staff should also be included here.

TRAVELING EXPENSES

The cost of the maintenance and transportation of the manager or staff members of the restaurant when they are traveling on business is to be charged to this account in all cases except when traveling is done in connection with business promotion in which case the expense is charged to "Advertising and Promotion."

INSURANCE—GENERAL

All types of insurance costs other than those included as "employee benefits" and fire and extended coverage on the premises and contents should be charged to this account. The types of insurance costs included here would be

Burglary, holdup, forgery, fraud, robbery
Fidelity Bonds
Public, boiler and elevator Liability
Food poisoning
Dram shop act
Use and occupancy
Lost or damaged articles
Partners' or officers' life insurance—(if payable to the restaurant company).

FEES TO CREDIT ORGANIZATIONS

In the past few years the influence of credit card operations on sales has been felt by many restaurants in that they have resulted in a sizable increase of extension of credit to customers. Many of these customers have obtained credentials from such organizations as American Express Company, Diner's Club and Carte Blanche, and now the banks around the country are rapidly entering this field. These credit organizations charge a fee for central billing and collection of credit accounts, which they deduct from their remittances.

Although many restaurant men feel that these fees are in the nature of a sales promotion cost, they actually are the result of adopting an administrative policy to recognize these cards. For this reason, fees to credit organizations are considered as an administrative expense, akin to a billing and collection fee, and are included in this group of expenses in the profit and loss statement.

COLLECTION FEES

This account is charged with the cost of collecting customers' accounts, and collecting agency and attorneys fees, notary fees, and the cost of credit reports, etc.

PROVISION FOR DOUBTFUL ACCOUNTS

A charge sufficient to provide for the probable loss in collection of accounts, returned checks, and other receivables should be charged to this expense account, and the contra entry of a credit to a reserve for doubtful accounts should appear as a balance sheet item. If this reserve method is used any accounts written off will be charged against this reserve. If no reserve is used any accounts written off should be charged directly to this expense account.

CASH SHORTAGES

Cashiers' shortages not recovered should be charged to this account. If there is a cash overage, the account will, of course, show a credit balance and might, therefore, be transferred to the profit and loss statement as "other income."

CLAIMS AND DAMAGES PAID

Payments made for customers' property lost or damaged and not covered by insurance should be charged to this account.

PROFESSIONAL FEES

All legal fees and expenses, other than collection costs, the cost of public accountants services, the fees of a business engineering firm, and the cost of similar professional services should be charged here.

PROTECTIVE SERVICE

This account should be charged with the cost of any police and watchmen, fire or burglar alarm, armored car or special detective service. Fees for bank deposit pick-up such as is supplied on contract by Brink's Express will also be charged to this account.

FRANCHISE FEES AND ROYALTIES

Any royalties or franchise fees paid to organizations which have issued a license to the restaurant for the use of certain operating methods or sale of certain products under their patent, copyright, or control should be charged in this category.

SALES TAXES

Any sales tax paid to a state or municipal government which has not been recovered from the customer should be charged here. If the restaurant chooses to absorb the sales tax in the price of meals or drinks at the bar, this is an administrative decision and, thus, this item becomes an administrative expense under the Uniform System.

PERSONNEL EXPENSES, HELP WANTED ADS, ETC.

With payroll costs and employee benefits becoming an increasingly major item of expense in restaurant operation, and with more government control on payrolls, the costs of operating the payroll department have also increased sufficiently to warrant many restaurants setting up a personnel office staff and a separate account for the expenses involved. The cost of employer investigations, health examinations, help-wanted advertising, personnel travel and other expenses in soliciting staff, etc. are to be charged to this account.

MISCELLANEOUS

This category is to take care of the relatively small charges for all items which are administrative or general in nature and are not included under any other captions in this section. For example, such items as the following would be included here:

    Car, bus or taxicab fares
    Bank charges
    Safe deposit box rentals
    Western Union time service

REPAIRS AND MAINTENANCE

Amounts

Painting and Decorating $
Repairs to — Dining Room Furniture
          Dishwashing and Sanitation Equipment
          Kitchen Equipment
          Office Equipment
          Refrigeration
          Air-conditioning
          Plumbing and Heating
          Electrical
          Elevators and Lifts
          Floors and Floor Coverings
          Buildings
          Gardening and Grounds Maintenance
          Parking Lot Repairs
Building Alterations not in the Nature of an Improvement
Plastering
Upholstering
Mending Curtains, Drapes and Hangings
Maintenance Contracts — Elevators
              Signs
              Office Machinery

TOTAL REPAIRS AND MAINTENANCE $

NOTE. These items are believed to be fully descriptive of the costs and expenses to be charged to this account and to be self-explanatory.

RENT OR OCCUPATION COSTS

Amounts

Rent — Minimum or Fixed Amount $
     Additional Percentage Rental   _____ $
Ground Rent
Real Estate Taxes
Personal Property Taxes
Other Municipal Taxes
Franchise Tax
Capital Stock Tax
Partnership or Corporation License Fees
Insurance on Building and Contents
Interest Paid

   Total Before Depreciation $

DEPRECIATION
   Buildings $
   Amortization of Leasehold
   Amortization of Leasehold Improvements
   Furniture, Fixtures and Equipment

   Total Depreciation $
TOTAL RENT OR OCCUPATION COSTS $

This group of expenses comprises the rental charge for any premises leased and such costs as fire and extended coverage insurance, real estate tax, personal property tax, sewer tax, interest on mortgages or other borrowings. In other words, these expenses, together with the depreciation charges, are the cost of presenting the premises to the management ready to operate. These are sometimes called "fixed charges" since their amount is usually determined by the financial setup of the restaurant and not by the trend of its business.

The specific costs included in this group will vary according to whether the premises are leased or owned and also according to whether the amount invested in the business is represented by borrowed capital or equity money put up by the owners. Thus, these costs and expenses will show a wide variation in amount and ratio to sales since they depend on how the restaurant is financed and, if it is operated on rented premises, what the rental terms of the lease provide.

RENT

Rental paid to the lessor for the use of the premises is charged here. If it is a percentage lease it may be desirable to show the minimum rental and the additional percentage rental separately in the profit and loss statement. If the rent is for the ground only the account should be titled "Ground Rent."

Any payments on local taxes, insurance, etc., which must be made by the tenant under the terms of the lease should be shown separately and are not to be included in this amount.

PROPERTY TAXES, PROPERTY INSURANCE AND INTEREST

Because many of the items included in this group are paid in a lump sum for a six-month period, a year, or in the case of insurance, for a three or five-year period, the charge to expense should be prorated so that each month or year bears its proportionate share of the cost. If these items are charged to expense in the month in which they are paid the operating result shown in the profit and loss statement will be distorted.

LOCAL PROPERTY TAXES

The items which are properly classified under this heading may be shown separately on the profit and loss statement, if desired, and they may be further analyzed under the headings which follow.

REAL ESTATE TAXES

Taxes assessed on the land and buildings by a state, county, or city government will be included in this classification if they are to be paid by the lessee or if the property is owned by the restaurant operator.

Special assessments for public improvements are ordinarily considered an increase in the value of the property, and this type of tax should not be included under this heading, but charged to the land account.

PERSONAL PROPERTY TAXES

Taxes assessed on personal property and payable by the restaurant operator are charged to this account.

SEWER TAX

Charges made by a municipality for the use of sewers are to be charged here.

Some municipalities may have a similar form of property service tax in which case the amount assessed and payable by the restaurant operator will be charged to the local property tax group, preferredly as a separate item in the profit and loss statement.

FRANCHISE OR CAPITAL STOCK TAXES
CORPORATION OR PARTNERSHIP LICENSES

This account will be charged with the taxes assessed for the privilege of doing business, such as the franchise tax, capital stock tax, or any partnership or corporation license fee.

INSURANCE ON BUILDING AND CONTENTS

The cost of insurance coverage on the buildings and contents against damage or destruction by fire, water, tornado, sprinkler leakage, boiler explosion, plate glass breakage, etc., is properly charged to this account if it is to be paid by the restaurant operator.

INTEREST PAID

Charges to this account include interest expense on bonds, mortgages, notes, equipment contracts, taxes in arrears, loans, and any other like indebtedness incurred by the operator in financing his restaurant. It is sometimes advisable to show the amount of interest on each class of obligation separately.

DEPRECIATION

Although the costs of operation included under this heading are really a part of the Rent or Occupation Costs group they are classified separately because they represent the decrease in the value of assets resulting from use and obsolescence. Since these assets have already been acquired and financed and no outlay of cash is required, it is of interest to know the result of the operation before deducting depreciation, and the profit and loss statement is designed to give this figure.

Depreciation is defined in Bulletin "F" issued by the U.S. Internal Revenue Service as "a reasonable allowance for the exhaustion, wear and tear of property used in the trade or business, including a reasonable allowance for obsolescence."

BUILDINGS

The estimated decrease in the value of the buildings used by the restaurant operator due to wear and tear and obsolescence should be charged to this account if they are owned by the restaurant.

AMORTIZATION OF LEASEHOLD

The costs of acquiring a lease and the expenses incidental thereto, originally charged to an asset account, should be extinguished proportionately over the remaining life of the lease by charges to this expense account.

AMORTIZATION OF LEASEHOLD IMPROVEMENTS

The costs of permanent improvements made to leased property, originally charged as an asset, should be extinguished by proportionate charges to this account, either over the remaining life of the lease or over the estimated useful life of the improvement, whichever is shorter.

FURNITURE, FIXTURES AND EQUIPMENT

The estimated decrease in the value of the furniture, fixtures and equipment resulting from wear and tear and obsolescence will be charged to this account.

This account should not include the depreciation on linens, china, glass, silver and similar operating equipment items which should be accounted for on a periodical inventory basis, as suggested in the "Direct Operating Expenses" category.

DEPRECIATION GUIDELINES

The 1958 edition of this book included excerpts from U. S. Treasury Department—Bureau of Internal Revenue Service Bulletin "F" which was last revised in 1942 and had been used as a guideline to the basis of depreciation on fixed assets. This bulletin is now out-dated and is no longer used as a guide to taxpayers and treasury agents. Meanwhile, many changes have been made in the regulations issued by the Bureau of Internal Revenue pertaining to the methods of calculation as well as to the bases (expressed as useful life) of depreciation. We suggest that on all questions of this type the restaurant man should consult his accountant or lawyer in deciding on the most advantageous method and procedure to follow.

Revenue Procedure 62-21 issued by the Internal Revenue Service in 1962 to aid taxpayers in the computation of depreciation allowances, outlined suggested useful lives for various types of depreciable fixed assets. The following excerpts from these guidelines that affect the Restaurant Industry are included here for your guidance.

GROUP ONE — GUIDELINES FOR DEPRECIABLE ASSETS, USED BY BUSINESS IN GENERAL

1. OFFICE FURNITURE, FIXTURES, MACHINES AND EQUIPMENT — 10 YEARS

Includes furniture and fixtures which are not a structural component of the building, and machines and equipment used in the preparation of papers or data; includes such assets as desks, files, safes, typewriters, accounting, calculating and data processing machines, communications, duplicating and copying equipment.

2. TRANSPORTATION EQUIPMENT

Includes the following types of transportation equipment:

(a)	Aircraft	6 years
(b)	Automobiles	3 years
(c)	Buses	9 years
(d)	General-Purpose Trucks	
	Light (less than 13,000 pounds)	4 years
	Heavy (13,000 pounds or more)	6 years

3. LAND IMPROVEMENTS   20 years

Includes land improvements such as paved surfaces, sidewalks, canals, waterways, drainage facilities and sewers, wharves, bridges, all fences except farm fences, landscaping, shrubbery and similar improvements.

4. BUILDINGS

Includes the structural shell of the building and all integral parts thereof. Includes equipment which services normal heating, plumbing, air-conditioning, fire prevention and power requirements, and equipment such as elevators and escalators.

Type of building	
Apartments	40 years
Garages	45 years
Hotels	40 years
Loft buildings	50 years
Office buildings	45 years
Stores	50 years
Warehouses	60 years

Excludes special-purpose structures which are an integral part of the production process and which, under normal practice, are replaced contemporaneously with the equipment which they house, support or serve.

5. SUBSIDIARY ASSETS

Includes crockery, glassware, linens and silverware and other subsidiary assets which are commonly and properly accounted for separately from those assets falling within guideline classes in Groups Two, Three and Four.

Where assets in this class are accounted for under a method of depreciation using a life expressed in terms of years, the life shall be determined according to the facts and circumstances.

GROUP TWO — GUIDELINES FOR NON-MANUFACTURING ACTIVITIES, EXCLUDING TRANSPORTATION, COMMUNICATIONS AND PUBLIC UTILITIES

In general, a single guideline class is specified for each industry included in this group. This single guideline class includes all depreciable property that is not covered by another guideline class. Thus, a single industry guideline class includes production machinery and equipment, power plant machinery and equipment, special equipment, and special purpose structures (as defined in Guidelines Class 4 under Group One).

The guideline classes in this group exclude depreciable assets covered under Group One.

8. WHOLESALE AND RETAIL TRADE   10 years

Includes purchasing, selling and brokerage activities at both wholesale and retail level, and related assembling, sorting and grading of goods.

Includes restaurants, cafes, coin-operated dispensing machines, and equipment of scrap metal brokers and of department stores (except office furniture and fixtures).

GROUP THREE — GUIDELINES FOR MANUFACTURING

The guideline classes in this group exclude depreciable assets covered under Group One.

7. FOOD AND KINDRED PRODUCTS   12 years

Includes the manufacture of foods and beverages, such as meat and dairy products; baked goods; canned, frozen and preserved products; confectionery and related products; and soft drinks and alcoholic beverages.

* * * * * * *

The above excerpts cover the items in the guidelines which may pertain to fixed assets commonly found in the restaurant business and pertain to suggested useful lives acceptable by the Internal Revenue Service under normal circumstances.

As to calculation methods, such as straight-line, declining balance, sum-of-the-digits, etc., and as to any unusual circumstances, we again advise the restaurant man to consult his accountant or lawyer in determining what is most advantageous for income tax purposes.

OTHER ADDITIONS TO AND DEDUCTIONS FROM NET PROFIT

Any income or expense items not applicable to the regular operation of the restaurant will be charged to this account. They would include:

Interest, Rentals, Dividends or Profits Earned on Outside Investments.
Profits or Losses on Sales of Investments.
Profits or Losses on Sales of Equipment.
Judgments or Settlement of Claims, (other than on lost or damaged articles).
Tax Refunds or Assessments Applying to Prior Years.

INCOME TAXES

Every profit making organization must pay income taxes on its taxable income and the amount of these taxes is as much a cost of doing business as any other expense item shown on the profit and loss statement. In the case of single proprietors and partnerships, it may not be practical to show these taxes on the restaurant operating statement as the individuals involved may have other items of taxable income or loss that will affect the amount of income tax to be paid. In corporation statements these taxes usually are included in the profit and loss statement.

Therefore, the item of income taxes, which are determined on the basis of net taxable profit, are included as the final deduction on the profit and loss statement in arriving at the net profit of the restaurant company.

Federal income taxes for the period covered by the profit and loss statement and based on the taxable profit of that period are charged to this account. Many states and some municipalities also have income taxes and the amounts of these taxes computed on the profit for the period of the statement are also charged here.

THE BALANCE SHEET
Sometimes Called The
STATEMENT OF ASSETS, LIABILITIES AND CAPITAL

A restaurant man's financial condition depends on many things such as the amount he can personally invest, his ability to obtain borrowed capital, the sternness or leniency of his creditors, his ability as an operator, and the opportunity to maintain a fair sales volume through location and local conditions. For this reason, it is important for him to have proper records from which he can prepare a statement of his assets. These, offset by a list of his liabilities, give the balance which represents the amount of capital investment he has in his business. It is this balance of assets versus liabilities and capital, which has given the name for the statement of financial position which is called "THE BALANCE SHEET."

Although the form of the balance sheet of a restaurant is made up in much the same manner as that of any other business, it reveals some major differences. For example, a restaurant ordinarily does not extend wide credit to its customers and thus does not have large sums tied up in accounts receivable, nor does it require a large investment in inventories. Instead, the usual restaurant balance sheet shows that most of the money is invested in fixed assets, such as land, building, furniture, equipment, leasehold and leasehold improvements. The working capital requirement is also smaller than that of a mercantile or manufacturing business, because, for the most part, restaurant sales are immediately realized in cash, and, since the restaurant operator may obtain credit in the payment of his bills, it is possible that he would make payment on some of the expenses for last month with the cash taken in today.

WORKING CAPITAL

Working capital is the excess of current assets (which are cash, receivables, marketable investments, inventories and prepaid expenses) over current liabilities (which are accounts payable, accrued expenses, current portion of loans, etc.).

The illustrative balance sheets in Part II of this book show working capital as follows:

Balance Sheet	Current Assets	Current Liabilities	Working Capital
Exhibit D	$ 23,600	$ 22,550	$ 950
Exhibit F	136,675	100,450	36,225
Exhibit H	183,025	192,025	(9,000)
Exhibit J	181,500	169,750	11,750
Exhibit L	27,475	28,265	(790)

In the restaurant operations used as examples in Exhibits D, F and J, the existence of a working capital balance indicates an ability to meet all current obligations from the proceeds of current assets. In Exhibits H and L, however, there are deficiencies of working capital despite the fact that in these examples the restaurants are meeting their obligations on time, taking advantage of cash discounts, etc. In fact, in Exhibit H you will note that cash on deposit represents 40% of the current assets and in Exhibit L it amounted to 68%. While these illustrations are not intended to represent average circumstances, they do indicate the fact that it is possible to operate in the restaurant business with a much smaller working capital than is usually the case in mercantile and manufacturing enterprises, which require larger sums to finance their accounts receivable and inventories.

THE CURRENT RATIO

A banker may, upon looking over a balance sheet, talk about the "current ratio," which is a term commonly used in discussing one's ability to meet obligations as they come due. The "current ratio" is arrived at by dividing the current assets by the current liabilities and in normal mercantile or manufacturing businesses the ratio of 2 to 1 — which means that there are two dollars in current assets for every dollar in current liabilities — would be considered a good liquid financial condition. However, creditors have come to rely more on the ability of debtors to pay their obligations out of the proceeds of current operations and less upon the debtor's ability to pay in case of liquidation. This may also affect the banker's analysis of financial condition because the restaurant business provides a steady flow of cash from current operations.

The current ratios for the balance sheets used in Part II of this book are calculated as follows:

Balance Sheet	Current Assets	Current Liabilities	Current Ratio of Current Assets to Current Liabilities
Exhibit D	$ 23,600	$ 22,500	1.05 to 1
Exhibit F	136,675	100,450	1.36 to 1
Exhibit H	183,025	192,025	.95 to 1
Exhibit J	181,500	169,750	1.07 to 1
Exhibit L	27,475	28,265	.97 to 1

Again we stress that these illustrations are not intended to be typical, nor do we advocate operating a business on a small cash margin, for to do this successfully there must be relative certainty that business will continue to be good and that the future income will be sufficient to meet today's obligations. The high mortality rate in the restaurant business is largely due to the fact that many restaurant operators try to conduct their establishments with insufficient capital and in this situation they are often squeezed to the point where they cannot meet their obligations as they become due.

The balance sheet accounts which a restaurant might have are shown in Exhibit B. Not all of these accounts will be necessary in every restaurant and some restaurants will have other accounts which are not listed. This balance sheet is outlined in a form that reflects the recommendations of the American Institute of Certified Public Accountants with respects to the classification of current assets and current liabilities as set forth in their Accounting Research Bulletin No. 43, Chapter 3A.

BALANCE SHEET
NAME OF RESTAURANT COMPANY
AS AT (Insert Date)

ASSETS

CURRENT ASSETS
    Cash on Hand $
    Cash in Bank   ———————— $

    Accounts Receivable — Customers $
                           Credit Cards
                           Employees
                           Other   ————————

       Total Receivables $
    Deduct reserve for doubtful accounts   ————————

    Deposits, Utility
    Inventories — Food $
                    Beverages
                    Cigar Stand
                    Supplies   ————————
    Marketable Securities
    Prepaid Expenses   ————————
       Total Current Assets $

DUE FROM OFFICERS, STOCKHOLDERS, PARTNERS
DUE FROM AFFILIATED OR ASSOCIATED COMPANIES
FUNDS IN HANDS OF TRUSTEE — RESTRICTED
RENTAL DEPOSIT
CASH SURRENDER VALUE OF LIFE INSURANCE
INVESTMENTS — NOT MARKETABLE AND NON-CURRENT

FIXED ASSETS
    Land $
    Buildings $
    Deduct Accumulated Depreciation   ————————
    Leasehold and Leasehold Improvements $
    Deduct Accumulated Amortization   ————————
    Furniture, Fixtures and Equipment $
    Deduct Accumulated Depreciation   ————————
    Linens, China, Glass, Silver, Utensils, Uniforms   ————————
        Net Book Value of Fixed Assets

DEFERRED EXPENSES
    Organization and Preopening Expense $
    Bond Discount and Loan Expense
    Cost of Improvements in Progress   ————————

OTHER ASSETS
    Amount Paid for Goodwill $
    Cost of Bar License
    Deposit on Franchise or Royalty Contract, etc.   ———————— $

TOTAL ASSETS

LIABILITIES AND CAPITAL

CURRENT LIABILITIES
    Accounts Payable to Trade Creditors $
    Accounts Payable to Others
    Notes Payable to Banks
    Notes or Contracts Payable on Equipment, etc.
    Taxes Collected
    Employees' Savings Plan Deposits
    Deposits on Banquets and Parties
    Income Tax—State and Federal
    Accrued Expenses—Payroll $
                Social Security Taxes
                Real Estate and Personal
                  Property Taxes
                Rent
                Interest
                Utilities
                Other   _____
    Portion of Long-Term Loans due within
      One Year
    Dividends Declared and Payable   _____
      Total Current Liabilities $
DUE TO OFFICERS, STOCKHOLDERS, PARTNERS
DUE TO AFFILIATED OR ASSOCIATED COMPANIES
LONG-TERM LOANS (MORTGAGES, BOND ISSUES,
    CONTRACTS, NOTES)
    Indicate each Loan Separately—
      Describe Terms and Conditions $
    Deduct Portion due within One Year and
      shown as Current Liability   _____

RESERVES
    Name here the Contingency covered by Reserve

CAPITAL (If a Corporation)
    Capital Stock
      Describe each type of Stock, Shares Authorized
        and Issued, Stated Value per Share $
      Surplus (Usually the Retained Earnings)   _____
      Total Capital

NET WORTH (If an Individual Proprietor or Partnership)
    Proprietor's Account $
    Partner A
    Partner B, etc.   _____
      Total Net Worth
TOTAL LIABILITIES AND CAPITAL $

ASSETS

CURRENT ASSETS

The current asset accounts include cash, receivables, inventories of saleable merchandise and supplies, utility deposits, prepaid expenses, and investments of funds which temporarily are not needed in the conduct of the business.

CASH ON HAND

This account is charged with the house·funds, house banks, or change funds in the custody of cashiers or other employees of the restaurant.

If all cash receipts are deposited daily, as advocated later in this book, the undeposited receipts which may temporarily be on hand at the end of the month will be shown under, "Cash On Deposit" as a "deposit in transit."

CASH ON DEPOSIT

If more than one bank account is maintained, it is advisable that each be shown separately, either on the face of the balance sheet itself or in a separate supporting schedule. Each bank account will, of course, require a separate account in the accounting records of the restaurant.

If cash is deposited in a special account to be used for a specific purpose and not in the ordinary course of business, and, thus, is not available for the liquidation of current liabilities, the account should not be included in the current assets in the balance sheet but should be shown under a separate heading following the total of these assets. Such restricted cash might be deposited to a sinking fund required under a mortgage or put in escrow on a purchase of land or other capital investment.

RECEIVABLES

This account should be charged with all amounts due from customers on open account. It is advisable to separate the amounts due to extension of credit to regular customers from those which arise from the policy of accepting credit cards. Employees and officers current balances due, rentals or commissions from concessionaires, and accounts arising from temporary loans to employees, all come under this category. Each class of account should, however, be shown separately on the balance sheet or in a supporting schedule.

In the event the restaurant should have a current obligation due it covered by a note, it should be listed in a separate "Notes Receivable" account and the amount of the note shown as a separate item with the receivables.

Notes and accounts due from stockholders, officers, employees, and affiliated or associated enterprises should not be included under this caption, but should be shown separately on the balance sheet below the total of current assets.

The detail of accounts and notes receivable, showing the names of the debtor, the age of the account, and the individual amounts due, may be shown in a supporting schedule to the balance sheet. The extent of this detail will depend on the individual requirements of the persons for whom the statement is prepared.

RESERVE FOR DOUBTFUL ACCOUNTS

If a policy of providing a reserve for probable losses in the collection of existing receivables is adopted, this account should be credited with an amount sufficient to cover accounts that are considered doubtful. If this is done monthly, the charge to expense, which is to be credited to this account, is usually based on past experience and the amount is adjusted to the actual collectibility of the accounts at the end of the year.

When this method is used, any uncollectible accounts should be charged to the reserve account when they are written off.

These reserve provisions are adjustments that the bookkeeper will make by journal entry from time to time.

DEPOSITS

Many restaurants are required to make deposits on certain of their utility contracts, such as water, gas, electricity, telephone, etc., and an account should be opened for each. The amounts are shown as current assets since they are offset by the liability for these utility costs.

Accounts representing deposits on airline credit cards or on purchase committments which have not yet become actual liabilities should be included in this section of the balance sheet.

INVENTORIES

A separate account should be kept for each type of inventory. The food inventory will include the cost of provisions that are on hand in the storeroom, ice boxes, pantries, kitchens and in storage warehouses. The beverage inventory will include stock at the bars or in the wine cellar and that in warehouses. There should be other inventory accounts for the cigar stand and other merchandise intended for sale and for supplies used in the business, such as cleaning supplies, stationery, guests supplies, mechanical supplies, etc.

Because of the rapid turnover of these items it is usual to value the inventories of a restaurant at the latest cost of each item.

INVENTORY TURNOVER

The rate of inventory turnover, which is an index often used in food and beverage control to determine the efficiency of operation, is arrived at by dividing the gross cost by the average inventory.

The following calculations, taken from the statements included in this book, will illustrate how the food turnover is calculated:

Food Operation	Food Cost Before Employees' Meals	Average Food Inventory	Annual Inventory Turnover
Exhibit C	$132,000	$ 3,150	42 Times
Exhibit E	466,875	8,750	53 Times
Exhibit G	828,950	21,725	38 Times
Exhibit I	690,000	16,750	41 Times
Exhibit K	132,500	1,850	72 Times

The inventory turnover on beverages is similarly calculated as follows:

Beverage Operation	Beverage Cost	Average Beverage Inventory	Annual Inventory Turnover
Exhibit E	$121,875	$18,375	6.6 Times
Exhibit G	202,500	17,500	11.6 Times

Because in a beverage operation a relatively larger stock must be maintained than in the food operation, the beverage inventory turnover is usually much smaller than is shown for a food operation.

Linens, china, glass, silver, utensils and uniforms are classified as "fixed assets" under the Uniform System of Accounts for Restaurants. For that reason, any amounts shown in the inventory accounts that are kept on these items are not included here with the current assets, but are shown in the later section of the balance sheet devoted to fixed assets.

MARKETABLE SECURITIES

Only those investments which are purchased to make temporary use of surplus funds and which can readily be converted into cash should be included in this current asset account. Any accrued interest receivable on bonds or notes included in this group should be charged to a separate account and the amount should also be included, as a separate item, under this category of current assets. It is advisable to indicate the basis of value on these investments, usually their cost or purchase price.

Investments of a permanent nature should be shown separately on the balance sheet after the total of current assets.

PREPAID EXPENSES

A separate account should be kept for each prepaid expense item. If they are not numerous they might be listed on the face of the balance sheet or they may be shown in more detail in a supporting schedule. This group of assets includes such items as unexpired insurance premiums, prepaid interest, rent, taxes and licenses.

TOTAL CURRENT ASSETS

The balance sheet should show a total of current assets so that the operator will know the amount of assets used in the direct operation of the business and can easily arrive at the liquid or "current" position of the company in determining its "working capital" and "current ratio," which are important factors in indicating the ability to meet current bills.

DUE FROM OFFICERS, STOCKHOLDERS, PARTNERS

As explained under the caption "Receivables," the amounts due from officers, stockholders, partners, and employees, including loans or notes and accrued interest thereon, that are not currently collectible in the ordinary course of business, should be shown as separate items below the total of current assets on the balance sheet.

DUE FROM AFFILIATED OR ASSOCIATED COMPANIES

The same treatment should be given to amounts due from affiliated or associated companies as is suggested for amounts due from officers, stockholders, partners, and employees.

FUNDS IN HANDS OF TRUSTEE—RESTRICTED

Funds deposited in the hands of a trustee or placed in escrow, which are thus restricted in nature and not available for the payment of liabilities incurred in the ordinary daily course of business, should be shown separately on the balance sheet below the total of current assets.

If, however, such cash is deposited with trustees for the payment of current obligations which are shown in the current liability section of the balance sheet, they may be shown as current assets. Such items may be current interest and principal payments on a loan, real estate taxes, etc.

RENTAL DEPOSIT

In many cases a restaurant lease will call for the deposit of cash or marketable investments as security for the rental due and the proper performance of other stated terms. Thus, the amount deposited is no longer available to the restaurant operator in the conduct of his business, and it must be shown separately on the balance sheet below the total of current assets.

If this deposit should draw interest payable to the operator, the amount of this accrued interest receivable may be shown as a current asset.

CASH SURRENDER VALUE OF LIFE INSURANCE

In cases where insurance is carried on the lives of officers, partners, or key employees and the restaurant is the beneficiary under the policy, the cash surrender value as shown by the policy should be accrued and set up in an account, the amount of which will be shown under a separate caption on the balance sheet below the total of current assets.

Although it is true that these policies might be cashed at any time it is not the usual intent in the ordinary course of business and for this reason this item is not considered to be a current asset.

INVESTMENTS—NON-CURRENT

Investments made in affiliated or associated companies or land, securities or other items purchased for permanent investment should be included in this category under a separate heading below the total of current assets.

FIXED ASSETS

This class of assets, which are to be shown as a separate group on the balance sheet below the total of current assets, includes such items used in the business as land, buildings, furniture, fixtures and equipment, automobiles and trucks, and unamortized value of leaseholds and leasehold improvements. There should be a separate account for each type of fixed asset.

The basis of value, whether at cost or appraised value, etc., should be shown on the face of the balance sheet. Buildings, furniture, fixtures and equipment, automobiles and trucks are subject to evaluation based on their age and the estimate of the extent of their useful life that has expired. This is done by creating a depreciation reserve account for each type, which is to be deducted from the value of the asset on the balance sheet. In the case of a leasehold or leasehold improvement, the value decreases as the lease expires and this decrease in value is also reflected in a reserve for amortization which is deducted from the respective asset to reflect the extent to which its value has been charged to operations. Thus, the amount of the asset account minus the amount of its accumulated depreciation or amortization leaves the net asset value remaining to be charged to future operations in the ordinary course of business.

These reserves are merely a means of spreading the cost of the asset over the term of its useful life and they are not an attempt to establish the true or saleable value of the asset at any given time. Thus, these accounts reflect what is known as a "book value" which is not to be confused with actual value.

The accounts representing asset values of linen, china, glass, silver, utensils and uniforms are also to be included under fixed assets. As previously mentioned in the section of this text devoted to The Profit And Loss Statement, these items may or may not be accounted for by periodical inventories. In smaller restaurants the original investment is often included in the total of the furniture and fixtures account, and any replacements are charged to operating expense as they are purchased.

DEFERRED EXPENSES

Deferred expenses are to be shown on the balance sheet following the total of fixed assets. They are expenditures made which have no recoverable value or which will subsequently be charged to a fixed asset account. They include such items as organization or preopening expenses, bond discount and loan expense, or the cost of improvements in progress and not yet put into operation.

OTHER ASSETS

Other assets include items that cannot readily be included under any other grouping on the balance sheet. They are usually shown as the last item on the asset side of this statement, and their nature should be clearly shown on the face of the balance sheet. They include such items as good-will, cost of bar and liquor license, (in many states where licenses are restricted in number it is often necessary to purchase an existing license) or a deposit on a franchise or royalty contract.

LIABILITIES AND CAPITAL

CURRENT LIABILITIES

The current liability section of the balance sheet includes such items as bank overdrafts, short term loans from banks and other loans covered by notes, open accounts payable to trade creditors and others, taxes collected from customers and employees payable to federal or governmental agencies, deposits collected to apply on future sales commitments, accrued expenses, and the portion of long term liabilities that are due within one year of the balance sheet date.

ACCOUNTS PAYABLE — TRADE CREDITORS

Trade creditors are those from whom the restaurant man receives goods or services in the ordinary course of business. The total of the unpaid invoices due to these creditors is usually the item of greatest interest to a restaurant operator and thus it is the first item in the current liability section.

Amounts due to affiliated or associated companies may be included under this heading if they are minor in amount and are paid currently; otherwise, they should be shown separately on the balance sheet below the total of current liabilities.

ACCOUNTS PAYABLE — TO OTHERS

Accounts due to concessionaires representing collections from customers or extraordinarily large open accounts, such as might result from purchases of equipment, etc., should be shown separately on the balance sheet.

NOTES PAYABLE TO BANKS

This account should include short term notes due to banks. If there are additional short term notes on loans from others, they should be described and shown separately.

NOTES OR CONTRACTS PAYABLE ON EQUIPMENT, ETC.

Short term notes or contracts for the purchase of equipment or construction should be shown as a separate item on the balance sheet, since these are usually liabilities which do not arise in the ordinary course of business.

TAXES COLLECTED

All taxes collected from customers and employees and payable to federal or local governmental agencies should be shown under this heading and preferably either detailed on the face of the balance sheet or in a separate supporting schedule. These items include the following:

Collected from Customers

Sales Tax
Excise Tax on Jewelry, etc.

Collected from Employees

Federal Insurance Contributions Act Tax
Federal Income Tax Withholding
State Unemployment or Income Tax (where collected)

In some instances the restaurant also collects the union dues and similar items payable to other than governmental agencies in which case the liability for this item is usually included in this group.

EMPLOYEES SAVINGS BOND DEPOSITS

Where the restaurant has instituted a U.S. Savings Bond plan for its employees, the amount collected should be credited to this account and the bonds purchased for them charged to it.

Some restaurants attempt to control uniforms, badges, and other similar articles put into the custody of employees by obtaining a deposit for them, to be returned when the article is turned in. These deposits should also appear as a current liability on the balance sheet.

DEPOSITS ON BANQUETS AND PARTIES

Deposits made by customers to apply on future sales should be credited to a separate account on the books and shown as a current liability which will be offset when the customer is served.

INCOME TAX—STATE AND FEDERAL

It is preferable to show the estimated federal and state income taxes, as calculated in the tax returns filed, as a separate item in the current liability section. This total includes the unpaid income taxes for the current year and for any preceding periods.

Income taxes are a cost of doing business and many restaurants, for this reason, estimate these taxes monthly and adjust the estimated amount to the actual calculations on their returns at the end of the year.

ACCRUED EXPENSES

In many instances, expenses are incurred for a period of operation and are not payable until after the balance sheet date. Therefore, the amount of these expenses which applies to the period up to the balance sheet date is an actual current liability and should be recorded, not only to show the true picture of financial condition but also in order to charge each operating period with its proper proportion of these costs of doing business. These are called "accrued expenses" and they include:

Payroll
Social Security Taxes
    Federal Insurance Contributions Act
    Federal Unemployment
    State Unemployment
Rent
Franchise Fees
Interest (preferably showing interest on each type of loan or note separately)
Utilities
    Electricity
    Gas
    Water
    Steam
    Telephone

All of these accounts should be shown in one group in the current liability section and either detailed on the face of the balance sheet or listed in a supporting schedule.

Smaller restaurants may not find it practical to go to the trouble of making these accrual entries on the theory that the amounts involved are comparatively small and their omission will not seriously distort the figures on the profit and loss statement. This is a matter of judgment and the individual restaurant man must decide it for himself.

PORTION OF LONG TERM LOANS DUE WITHIN ONE YEAR

Because the total of current liabilities should include all obligations due within one year, it is preferable that the principal payments due the next year on any mortgage, loan, or conditional sales contract be described and shown separately on the balance sheet under this heading. This division will not necessitate a separate account on the books for these current payments, as will be discussed later under the caption, "Long Term Loans."

DIVIDENDS DECLARED AND PAYABLE

Any dividends that have been declared by the board of directors of a restaurant corporation and that are unpaid at the balance sheet date should be set up in a separate account and included with the current liabilities on the balance sheet.

TOTAL CURRENT LIABILITIES

The balance sheet should show a total of current liabilities so that the operator may know what is immediately ahead in the matter of cash requirement and can easily determine the restaurant's ability to pay its bills as they become due by comparing this total with the total of current assets and, thus, determining the "current" position.

DUE TO OFFICERS, STOCKHOLDERS, PARTNERS

Loans and other amounts due to officers, stockholders, and partners that are not to be considered a part of equity capital and are not due at any specified date or that are otherwise considered to be non-current should be shown as separate items below the total of current liabilities in the balance sheet. If those accounts are covered by notes they should be so described.

DUE TO AFFILIATED OR ASSOCIATED COMPANIES

The same treatment should be given to amounts payable to affiliated or associated companies as is suggested for the amounts due to officers, stockholders, and partners.

LONG TERM LOANS

Each loan should be shown separately in this section below the total of current liabilities and described by its exact title, interest rate, and due date.

Any portion of these long term loans due within one year should be deducted from the total of the loan outstanding and shown as a current liability, as explained under, "Portion Of Long Term Loans Due Within One Year." The calculation of the current portion is made for statement purposes only and does not require any entries on the books of the restaurant.

RESERVES

It is sometimes advisable to provide a reserve for some contingency, such as taxes or damage claims in dispute, imminent reconstruction or unusual repairs, replacements of operating equipment, etc., and the amounts of these reserve accounts should be shown in the balance sheet under this caption. The reserves for bonuses withheld from service charges and for vacation pay, which are mentioned earlier in this text in the Profit and Loss section, should actually be shown as current liabilities since they are payable within the year.

The charges offsetting these reserves are usually not deductible for income tax purposes, and they are regarded as an apportionment of net worth or surplus rather than as an operating expense, as the expense is chargeable to operations when the actual liability is incurred.

CAPITAL
CAPITAL STOCK (If a Corporation)

Each class or type of capital stock should be shown separately in this section of the balance sheet. The number of shares authorized, issued and outstanding and the par or stated capital per share of stock should be indicated.

If the corporation should purchase some of its shares and hold them in its treasury for sale or re-issue, these shares should be shown as "Treasury Stock" and it is preferable that their cost be deducted from the total Capital Stock and Surplus at the bottom of this capital section of the balance sheet.

SURPLUS (Retained Earnings)

The amount of earnings retained and used in the business is usually called, "earned surplus." It is advisable that a separate account be used to accumulate these net earnings which have not been distributed to the shareholders and thus become a part of the equity capital invested in the business. Ordinarily the changes in the earned surplus account are shown on the face of the balance sheet or in a supporting schedule as follows:

Earned Surplus at beginning of the Year $
   Add
       Net Earnings — Per Profit and Loss Statement
         Total $

Deduct:
     Dividends (Give Date Payable)
Earned Surplus at End of the Year $

Sometimes there are transactions during the year, such as additional income tax assessments or refunds, etc., that should properly apply to a prior year and the amounts are large enough to distort the profit and loss statement for the current year. In these cases, some companies prefer to record the adjustment directly in the surplus account rather than in a current operating income or expense account and the analysis shown would be changed to show these additional adjustments.

Surplus arising from other than the profits realized in the ordinary course of business, such as from placing an appreciated appraised value of assets on the books or from the purchase of the company's own securities at a discount, should be properly designated as a separate item in the balance sheet. This type of surplus is often termed, "Capital Surplus" but it is better to describe its exact nature and source more fully.

NET WORTH (If Sole Proprietor Or Partnership)

The proprietor's net worth account will include his invested capital and earnings retained in the business at the balance sheet date. If the restaurant is operated as a partnership, it is preferable to show each partner's net worth amount separately on the face of the balance sheet.

A summary of the changes in the net worth accounts during the year can be shown on the face of the balance sheet, as illustrated in Exhibits D and F in Part II.

PART II

Examples Of
PROFIT AND LOSS STATEMENTS AND BALANCE SHEETS
Based On
THE UNIFORM SYSTEM OF ACCOUNTS FOR RESTAURANTS

To illustrate the practical application of the Uniform System of Accounts for Restaurants, this section is devoted to sample statements based on the actual operating figures of several restaurants which were included in the review made in preparing this text.

Although the amounts and ratios shown in these statements are based on actual results and thus are a true indication of what the sales, costs and profits are in these particular instances, they are not intended to be used as standards of operation. In any comparisons made, the major elements of operation depend on the local circumstances under which the restaurants compared operate, and they are affected by such things as the location, type of patronage, physical layout and facilities, local wage rates and labor conditions, rental, and other factors. Therefore, the exhibits in this section are intended only to show how the form of statement recommended under the Uniform System of Accounts for Restaurants can be applied. The restaurants were selected primarily to illustrate the versatility of the Uniform System of Accounts, and the results shown in the exhibits are by no means average for the restaurant business. In Appendix C you will find the eighth Annual Study of Restaurant Operations prepared under the direction of two partners of the firm of Horwath & Horwath.

OPERATING RATIOS

In making comparisons of the trends in the operating results of a restaurant between one period and another, or of the figures of one restaurant with another or with those in such studies as may be made available through group action, or the restaurant associations and publications, it will be found quite helpful to translate the dollar figures into percentages, or ratios to total sales.

A ratio is usually calculated and expressed as a percentage of sales by dividing the dollar amount of each item on the profit and loss statement by the dollar amount of sales and multiplying the result by 100. For example, in Exhibit C the food cost of $132,000 divided by the sales figure of $350,000 is .3771 which multiplied by 100 is 37.71%. Thus, the food cost is said to be 37.71 cents per dollar sale, or 37.71 per cent of food sales.

By using percentages or ratios to sales rather than dollar amounts a restaurant man is in a position to talk food costs, payroll costs and other operating expenses without revealing his volume of sales or any other amounts in dollars that might be considered confidential. The Uniform System promotes a set of common terms for the various expenses, and the use of percentages thus provides an advantageous means of communication whereby even direct competitors can help each other by an exchange of information.

Both the dollar amounts and the ratios or percentages are used in the illustration in Exhibit C. These ratios may also be used in comparing the operating results of one month or one year of operations with another, since the ratios are easier to keep in mind than the dollars and cents figures. Moreover, ratios indicate more clearly the relationship of the various expenses to the sales of each period, how fluctuations in sales volume affect the costs and the extent to which changes in costs affect the final profit figure.

EXHIBITS C AND D

Exhibit C is a Profit and Loss Statement in summary form and the figures used in this sample statement were compiled from the composite operating results of eighteen street location restaurants doing a food business only, and having a cigar counter at the cashier's stand. This statement outlines the major figures of operation that a smaller restaurant man should know about his business and it gives a complete picture of such an operation on only 23 lines.

The basic figure in this summary is that of food sales and all of the costs, expenses and profit figures are shown in their relation to these sales in the percentage column.

These restaurants did not calculate the cost of employees' meals for statement purposes, and thus the food cost is the gross cost or, "Cost of Food Consumed." The major other income item was the gross profit on the cigar counter. There was only a nominal cost for music and entertainment provided by wired music, and advertising and sales promotion expenses were relatively low as is usual in the smaller street restaurants.

This profit and loss statement contains no provisions for income taxes since this is an illustration of an operation by a sole proprietor.

Exhibit D shows the Balance Sheet based on the same composite figures for these eighteen restaurants and illustrates the form that such a statement of financial condition would take for a single proprietorship operating on a lease basis.

Exhibit C

PROFIT AND LOSS STATEMENT
USING COMPOSITE FIGURES OF EIGHTEEN RESTAURANTS
TABLE AND COUNTER SERVICE
YEAR ENDED DECEMBER 31, 19--

		Amounts	Percentages
FOOD SALES		$350,000	100.00%
COST OF FOOD CONSUMED		132,000	37.71
GROSS PROFIT		$218,000	62.29%
OTHER INCOME		2,100	.60
TOTAL INCOME		$220,100	62.89%
CONTROLLABLE EXPENSES			
Payroll		$111,000	31.72%
Payroll Taxes and Employee Benefits		12,250	3.50
Employees' Meals		Not Figured	—
Direct Operating Expenses			
Laundry and Linen Rentals	$2,450		
China, Glassware, Silver and Linen	3,150		
Cleaning and Cleaning Supplies	3,500		
Paper and Customer Supplies	4,900		
Other	3,500	17,500	5.00
Music and Entertainment		350	.10
Advertising and Promotion		3,500	1.00
Utilities		8,750	2.50
Administrative and General		8,400	2.40
Repairs and Maintenance		7,000	2.00
Total Controllable Expenses		$168,750	48.22%
PROFIT BEFORE RENT AND OCCUPATION COSTS		$ 51,350	14.67%
RENT OR OCCUPATION COSTS		21,700	6.20
PROFIT BEFORE DEPRECIATION		$ 29,650	8.47%
DEPRECIATION		9,800	2.80
PROFIT BEFORE INCOME TAXES		$ 19,850	5.67%

BALANCE SHEET
USING COMPOSITE FIGURES OF EIGHTEEN RESTAURANTS
TABLE AND COUNTER SERVICE
AS AT DECEMBER 31, 19--

ASSETS

CURRENT ASSETS
Change Funds	$ 900	
Cash on Deposit	12,750	$13,650
Accounts Receivable—Customers	$ 175	
—Credit Card	1,525	1,700
Inventories—Food	$ 3,150	
—Supplies	1,750	4,900
Deposits—Utilities		350
Prepaid Expenses		3,000
Total Current Assets		$23,600

FIXED ASSETS
Furniture and Fixtures	$62,000	
Deduct Depreciation Reserve	20,700	$41,300
Leasehold Improvements	$35,500	
Deduct Amortization Reserve	13,200	22,300
Operating Equipment—China, Glass, Silver		9,500
Total Fixed Assets		73,100
TOTAL ASSETS		$96,700

LIABILITIES AND CAPITAL

CURRENT LIABILITIES
Accounts Payable—Trade Creditors	$16,325	
Taxes Collected	2,025	
Accrued Expenses	4,200	
Total Current Liabilities		$22,550
EQUIPMENT CONTRACTS PAYABLE		10,350
NOTES PAYABLE—LONG-TERM		20,000
Total Liabilities		$52,900

CAPITAL
Proprietor's Account—January 1, 19--	$41,950	
Profit for Year 19---—Exhibit C	19,850	
Total	$61,800	
Cash Drawings for Year	18,000	
Proprietor's Account December 31, 19--		43,800
TOTAL LIABILITIES AND CAPITAL		$96,700

EXHIBITS E AND F

The figures used in Exhibit E, which is a Profit and Loss Statement in summary form, were taken from the actual operating results of a restaurant specializing in the service of steaks and chops. This time the statement shows both food and beverage sales as separate figures, since, in this instance, the beverage sales represent about 29% of the total gross volume of the restaurant and they make an important contribution to the profit potential.

The food and beverage costs are also segregated so that the individual cost and gross profit ratios can be determined.

Because this restaurant is in the nature of a "night club" or "cabaret" type of operation, the prices on the drink or wine lists have been set to show a 25% beverage cost. This is far lower than the experience ratio of the ordinary restaurant and is made possible by the fact that the major beverage sales are mixed drinks, on which the cost is lower than on beers and wines, and better prices are obtainable because of the entertainment furnished. Menu prices have resulted in a food cost of 37.5%, as compared with one at 37.71% shown in Exhibit C for the eighteen street restaurants.

Sales taxes are not a factor in this operating statement since they are collected from the customer and remitted to the government, and the restaurant acts only as the withholding agent for these taxes. If, for example, sales taxes on drinks served at the bar were to be absorbed by the restaurant, the amount of such taxes would appear as a part of administrative and general expenses. But in this instance all sales are made at menu or drink list prices plus sales taxes.

The other income includes a rental received from the coat and wash room concession, the gross profit on the cigar counter sales, and other miscellaneous items.

In Exhibit E a separate expense line is shown for employees' meals. In this and other instances where employees' meals cost is calculated and deducted from the cost of food consumed, it is well to show this expense separately on the profit and loss statement so that it is clear that the food cost figure is net after provision for the food served to employees and one can, at the same time, see the effect of this calculation in the total of controllable expenses. This is necessary for uniformity since, as has been stated previously, many restaurant operators do not go to the trouble of calculating and showing the cost of employees' meals.

In this particular restaurant there is no cover or minimum charge despite the fact that music and entertainment is provided during the cocktail, dinner, and supper hours. In restaurants where it is the operating policy to add a cover charge or to require a minimum charge to help defray the cost of music and entertainment, the income from this source would be added to the other income, preferably as a separate item in the statement, and by comparison with the music and entertainment costs would indicate the extent to which these costs are recovered from this source. In a cabaret or night club operation it is very seldom that the cover charges exceed the cost of entertainment.

The cost of music and entertainment is 6.22% of total food and beverage sales in this operation as compared with a cost of .10% shown in Exhibit C. Also the cost of advertising and sales promotion is 3.20% of sales in Exhibit E as compared with 1.00% in Exhibit C. This wide fluctuation is the reason why these two direct expense items have been singled out and are to be shown separately according to the Uniform System of Accounts for Restaurants.

Because of the difference in the type of operation of the restaurants involved, the ratios of direct operating expenses and administrative and general expenses are higher in Exhibit E than in Exhibit C and the ratios of payroll, employee relations, utilities, and repair expenses are lower.

Exhibit F is the Balance Sheet of this specialty restaurant, operated on a lease basis, and this statement also furnishes an example of a partnership. In this instance, one partner has a two-thirds interest and the other a one-third interest in the capital and profits. Because it is a partnership operation, the statements show no provision for federal or state income taxes.

PROFIT AND LOSS STATEMENT
RESTAURANT WITH BEVERAGE SALES AND ENTERTAINMENT
YEAR ENDED DECEMBER 31, 19--

	Amounts	Percentages
SALES		
Food	$1,200,000	71.11%
Beverages	487,500	28.89
Total Sales	$1,687,500	100.00%
COST OF SALES		
Food	$ 450,000	37.50%
Beverages	121,875	25.00
Total Cost of Sales	$ 571,875	33.89%
GROSS PROFIT	$1,115,625	66.11%
OTHER INCOME	10,125	.60
TOTAL INCOME	$1,125,750	66.71%
CONTROLLABLE EXPENSES		
Payroll	$ 491,050	29.10%
Payroll Taxes and Employee Benefits	48,750	2.89
Employees' Meals	16,875	1.01
Direct Operating Expenses	92,800	5.50
Music and Entertainment	105,000	6.22
Advertising and Promotion	54,000	3.20
Utilities	27,000	1.60
Administrative and General	78,300	4.64
Repairs and Maintenance	22,500	1.33
Total Controllable Expenses	$ 936,275	55.48%
PROFIT BEFORE RENT OR OCCUPATION COSTS	$ 189,475	11.23%
RENT OR OCCUPATION COSTS	81,500	4.83
PROFIT BEFORE DEPRECIATION	$ 107,975	6.40%
DEPRECIATION	26,325	1.56
PROFIT BEFORE INCOME TAX	$ 81,650	4.84%

BALANCE SHEET
RESTAURANT WITH BEVERAGE SALES AND ENTERTAINMENT
AS AT DECEMBER 31, 19--

ASSETS

CURRENT ASSETS			
House Funds	$ 2,750		
Continental—Illinois Bank & Trust Co.	28,625	$ 31,375	
Receivables			
Credit cards	$ 46,950		
Customers	15,875		
Advances to Employees	650		
Total Receivables	63,475		
Deduct Reserve for Doubtful Account	1,225	62,250	
Inventories			
Food	$ 8,750		
Beverages	18,375		
Supplies	1,850	28,975	
Prepaid Rent		3,750	
Prepaid Insurance, etc.		10,325	
Total Current Assets			$136,675

	Cost	Depreciation Reserve	Net Book Value	
FIXED ASSETS				
Dining Room Furnishings	$110,000	$ 52,325	$ 57,675	
Kitchen Equipment	75,000	36,750	38,250	
Other Furnishings	22,500	9,125	13,375	
Leasehold Improvements	65,000	32,500	32,500	
Automobiles	7,250	3,600	3,650	
Total Fixed Assets	$279,750	$134,300		145,450
TOTAL ASSETS				$282,125

LIABILITIES AND CAPITAL

CURRENT LIABILITIES		
Accounts Payable	$ 61,850	
Taxes Collected—Employees	9,200	
Sales Tax—State	4,275	
Accrued Expenses	25,125	
Total Current Liabilities		$100,450

	Partner A	Partner B	Total	
PARTNER'S CAPITAL				
Capital—January 1, 19--	$114,684	$ 57,341	$172,025	
Profit—Exhibit E	54,433	27,217	81,650	
Total	$169,117	$ 84,558	$253,675	
Drawings	48,000	24,000	72,000	
Capital—December 31, 19--	$121,117	$ 60,558		181,675
TOTAL LIABILITIES AND CAPITAL				$282,125

EXHIBITS G AND H

The figures used in this Profit and Loss Statement and Balance Sheet are those of a large restaurant that has several dining rooms and a bar and cocktail lounge. Dinner music is furnished, there are piped-in musical programs at off-hours, and television is provided at the bar.

In Exhibit G the application of the Summary Profit and Loss Statement is shown in the same manner as for the restaurant operations portrayed in Exhibits C and E. However, in this instance the details of the major groupings of controllable expenses and of rent and occupation costs are shown in supporting schedules. This shows the manner in which this more detailed information can be portrayed in a large restaurant that has its own bookkeeping staff.

This exhibit is also used to illustrate a comparative form of statement, and it indicates the use and advantages of a comparison of the figures for the current year with those of the preceding year.

In this instance you will note a slight drop in sales, about 2% in food and 5% in beverages, in the current year compared to the prior year. Despite this, payroll and related expenses went up 2.52 percentage points, due primarily to the effect of the Wage and Hour Law starting February 1, 1967. A tighter control on other expense categories offset the payroll increases to some extent, but could not prevent a decrease of 1.70 percentage points in operating profit before fixed charges.

Employees' meals were calculated at this restaurant, and the food cost is shown "Net After Employees' Meals" or as the "Cost of Food Sales." Employees' meals are shown as a separate item on the Profit and Loss Statement to indicate the circumstance.

Employee Benefits expenses in this operation are higher in ratio to sales than those shown for the restaurants in Exhibits C and E. The added fringe benefits for this operation are detailed in Schedule G-2.

Since this restaurant is operated by a corporation, the element of income taxes is shown in the Profit and Loss Statement before arriving at the net profit.

Exhibit H shows the Balance Sheet for this restaurant company, which is operated as leased property, and is an illustration of the corporation form of statement of financial condition. This statement also contains the liability for corporation income taxes, an example of the treatment of a mortgage loan on the parking lot, and an amount set up for the purchase of goodwill at the time the company took over the operation of this restaurant.

COMPARATIVE PROFIT AND LOSS STATEMENT
A LARGE RESTAURANT WITH BEVERAGE FACILITIES

	Amounts		Percentages	
	Current Year	Prior Year	Current Year	Prior Year
SALES				
Food	$2,025,000	$2,065,000	75.00%	74.41%
Beverages	675,000	710,000	25.00	25.59
Total Sales	$2,700,000	$2,775,000	100.00%	100.00%
COST OF SALES				
Food	$ 765,500	$ 775,000	37.80%	37.53%
Beverages	202,500	215,000	30.00	30.28
Total Cost of Sales	$ 968,000	$ 990,000	35.85%	35.68%
GROSS PROFIT	$1,732,000	$1,785,000	64.15%	64.32%
OTHER INCOME	20,500	22,200	.76	.80
TOTAL INCOME	$1,752,500	$1,807,200	64.91%	65.12%
CONTROLLABLE EXPENSES				
Payroll — Schedule G-1	$ 920,700	$ 888,775	34.10%	32.03%
Employee Benefits — Schedule G-2	108,000	99,525	4.00	3.59
Employees' Meals	63,450	64,100	2.35	2.31
Direct Operating Expenses — Schedule G-3	165,000	171,500	6.11	6.18
Music and Entertainment	13,500	15,600	.50	.56
Advertising and Promotion — Schedule G-4	47,250	58,275	1.75	2.10
Utilities — Schedule G-5	48,750	47,175	1.81	1.70
Administrative and General — Schedule G-6	94,500	104,150	3.50	3.75
Repairs and Maintenance	46,150	58,850	1.71	2.12
Total Controllable Expenses	$1,507,300	$1,507,950	55.83%	54.34%
PROFIT BEFORE RENT AND OCCUPATION COSTS	$ 245,200	$ 299,250	9.08%	10.78%
RENT AND OCCUPATION EXPENSES — Schedule G-7	105,250	104,000	3.90	3.75
PROFIT BEFORE DEPRECIATION	$ 139,950	$ 195,250	5.18%	7.03%
DEPRECIATION — Schedule G-7	44,350	44,675	1.64	1.61
PROFIT BEFORE INCOME TAX	$ 95,600	$ 150,575	3.54%	5.42%
INCOME TAX ESTIMATE	39,400	66,175	1.46	2.38
NET PROFIT — TO SURPLUS	$ 56,200	$ 84,400	2.08%	3.04%

PAYROLL
A LARGE RESTAURANT WITH BEVERAGE FACILITIES

	Current Year	Prior Year
SERVICE		
Headwaiter and Hostesses	$ 20,000	$ 22,500
Captains	27,000	27,500
Waiters and Waitresses	160,500	158,600
Bus Boys	55,850	49,600
Page Boys	5,000	4,800
Total Service	$268,350	$263,000
BARTENDERS	$ 47,825	$ 48,150
PREPARATION		
Chefs	$ 33,100	$ 33,500
Cooks	95,350	94,250
Bakers	24,800	23,800
Butchers	22,200	20,200
Vegetable Preparation	10,800	7,800
Pantry	44,000	42,500
Total Preparation	$230,250	$222,050
SANITATION		
Steward	5,600	5,250
Dishwashers and potwashers	90,300	79,150
Kitchen Men	12,025	10,325
Cleaners	13,850	12,125
Total Sanitation	$121,775	$106,850
ADMINISTRATIVE AND GENERAL		
Executives and Manager's Office	$133,500	$136,000
Accounting Office	32,250	30,750
Personnel Office and Payroll	12,500	12,500
Cashiers and Checkers	32,400	30,550
Telephone and Timekeeping	9,450	8,500
Storeroom and Receiving	12,900	11,775
Engineer and Assistants	15,700	15,250
Watchmen	3,800	3,400
Total Administrative and General	$252,500	$248,725
TOTAL PAYROLL – TO EXHIBIT G	$920,700	$888,775

EMPLOYEE BENEFITS
A LARGE RESTAURANT WITH BEVERAGE FACILITIES

	Current Year	Prior Year
Federal Insurance Compensation Act	$ 26,625	$ 21,350
Federal Unemployment Tax	2,450	2,400
State Unemployment Tax	13,800	13,200
Union Employees' Pension Fund	17,875	16,750
Union Employees' Insurance Fund	24,300	23,900
Workmen's Compensation Insurance	12,500	12,000
Group Insurance	500	475
Employees' Health and Welfare Plan	8,100	7,700
Disability Insurance	1,850	1,750
TOTAL EMPLOYEE BENEFITS—TO EXHIBIT G	$108,000	$ 99,525

DIRECT OPERATING EXPENSES
A LARGE RESTAURANT WITH BEVERAGE FACILITIES

	Current Year	Prior Year
Uniforms	$ 4,675	$ 4,200
Laundry and Linen Rental	41,625	44,400
China and Glassware	26,750	28,450
Silverware	4,700	5,800
Kitchen Utensils	2,550	4,000
Kitchen Fuel	9,000	9,200
Cleaning Supplies	19,425	20,350
Paper Supplies	6,600	7,100
Guest Supplies	2,900	3,200
Bar Expense	1,550	1,800
Menus and Wine Lists	5,200	6,000
Contract Cleaning	4,800	4,800
Exterminating	1,500	1,500
Flowers and Decorations	3,750	3,050
Auto Expense	3,525	2,975
Parking Lot Expense	10,500	9,500
Licenses	3,600	3,750
Banquet Expense	10,850	9,325
Miscellaneous	1,500	2,100
TOTAL DIRECT EXPENSES—TO EXHIBIT G	$165,000	$171,500

ADVERTISING AND SALES PROMOTION
A LARGE RESTAURANT WITH BEVERAGE FACILITIES

	Current Year	Prior Year
Newspapers and Magazines	$12,225	$13,250
Direct Mail, Circulars, etc.	6,000	7,500
Advertising Agency Fees	3,400	4,100
Outdoor Signs	4,800	4,950
Radio and Television	10,500	14,025
Programs and Directories	1,500	1,425
Prizes and Favors	2,600	3,500
Donations	4,175	6,250
Entertainment and Sales Promotion	2,050	3,275
TOTAL ADVERTISING AND SALES PROMOTION — TO EXHIBIT G	$47,250	$58,275

UTILITIES
A LARGE RESTAURANT WITH BEVERAGE FACILITIES

	Current Year	Prior Year
Electricity	$19,050	$18,775
Electric Bulbs	650	600
Water	4,200	4,050
Waste Removal	4,800	4,800
Heat	17,750	17,000
Engineer's Supplies	2,100	1,800
Miscellaneous	200	150
TOTAL UTILITIES — TO EXHIBIT G	$48,750	$47,175

ADMINISTRATIVE AND GENERAL EXPENSES
A LARGE RESTAURANT WITH BEVERAGE FACILITIES

	Current Year	Prior Year
Printing, Stationery and Office Supplies	$ 6,775	$ 7,950
Data Processing Costs	18,650	18,450
Postage	1,750	2,500
Telephone	6,225	8,100
Dues and Subscriptions	2,750	3,150
Traveling Expenses	5,150	5,750
Insurance—General	17,500	18,350
Fees on Credit Card Accounts	7,800	7,250
Provision for Doubtful Accounts	775	850
Cash Shortages	800	1,050
Professional Fees—Legal and Accounting	14,000	17,725
Protective and Bank Pick-up	6,000	6,000
City Sales Tax	2,700	2,775
Miscellaneous	3,625	4,250
TOTAL ADMINISTRATIVE EXPENSES—TO EXHIBIT G	$94,500	$104,150

RENT OR OCCUPATION COSTS
A LARGE RESTAURANT WITH BEVERAGE FACILITIES

	Current Year	Prior Year
Rent	$ 60,000	$ 60,000
Real Estate and Personal Property Tax	26,875	25,350
Sewer Tax	1,200	1,200
Franchise Tax	4,500	4,200
Insurance on Property	6,800	6,650
Interest	5,875	6,600
TOTAL BEFORE DEPRECIATION—TO EXHIBIT G	$105,250	$104,000
DEPRECIATION AND AMORTIZATION		
Parking Lot Improvements	$ 3,750	$ 3,750
Leasehold Improvements	3,200	3,150
Furniture, Fixtures and Equipment	28,435	29,060
Air-Conditioning and Refrigeration	6,025	6,025
Automobiles	2,500	2,250
Mortgage Expense Amortization	440	440
TOTAL DEPRECIATION, ETC.—TO EXHIBIT G	$ 44,350	$ 44,675
TOTAL RENT AND OCCUPATION COSTS	$149,600	$148,675

BALANCE SHEET

A LARGE RESTAURANT WITH BEVERAGE FACILITIES
AS AT DECEMBER 31, 19

ASSETS

CURRENT ASSETS

Cash

Change Funds	$ 4,125	
On Deposit	73,650	
Total Cash		$ 77,750

Accounts Receivable

Customers	$ 36,250	
Credit Card Accounts	7,100	
Other	3,250	
Employees' Loans and Advances	2,150	
Total Receivables	$ 48,750	
Deduct — Reserve for Doubtful Accounts	1,175	
Net Accounts Receivable		47,575

Inventories

Food	$ 21,725	
Beverages	17,500	
Cigars, Cigarettes, Candy, etc.	1,500	
Supplies	4,750	
Total Inventories		45,475

Prepaid Expenses

Insurance, Taxes and Licenses		12,225
Total Current Assets		$183,025

FIXED ASSETS

Parking Lot		$120,000
Land Improvements	$ 37,500	
Deduct Depreciation Reserve	7,500	30,000
Leasehold Improvements	$ 64,350	
Deduct — Amortization	25,850	38,500
Furniture, Fixtures and Equipment	$365,000	
Deduct Depreciation Reserve	167,500	197,500
Air Conditioning and Refrigeration	$ 90,450	
Deduct Depreciation Reserve	36,250	54,200
Automobiles	$ 7,500	
Deduct Depreciation Reserve	5,000	2,500
Glassware, Crockery and Silver		31,350
Total Fixed Assets		474,050

DEFERRED CHARGES

Mortgage Expense	$ 3,510	
Advertising Program Prepaid	4,200	
Total Deferred Charges		7,710

GOODWILL 80,000

TOTAL ASSETS $744,785

LIABILITIES AND CAPITAL

CURRENT LIABILITIES

Accounts Payable — Trade Creditors		$ 82,600
Taxes Collected — Employees	$ 12,325	
Sales Taxes	5,000	17,325
Federal Income Tax		39,400
Accrued Expenses		
Rent	$ 5,000	
Payroll	16,800	
Social Security Taxes	6,250	
Interest on Loan		
Sewer Tax	550	
Water	850	
Steam	1,300	
Gas	325	
Electricity	550	
Real Estate and Personal Property Taxes	8,375	
Other	1,700	
Total Accrued Expenses		41,700
Current Portion — Mortgage Loan		11,000
Total Current Liabilities		$192,025

MORTGAGE LOAN ON REAL ESTATE — 6½%

Due September 30, 1975	$ 85,250	
Deduct Amount Due Within One Year	11,000	
Balance Due Long-Term		74,250

CAPITAL

Capital Stock		
2,500 Shares No-Par Common — Stated Value		$250,000
Surplus		
Retained Earnings — January 1, 19	$209,810	
Net Profit — Exhibit G	56,200	
Total	$266,010	
Dividends Paid	37,500	
Retained Earnings — December 31, 19		228,510
Total Capital		478,510

TOTAL LIABILITIES AND CAPITAL	$744,785

EXHIBITS I AND J

Exhibit I shows how the profit and loss statement prepared under The Uniform System of Accounts for Restaurants appears for a large restaurant selling food only and having table, counter and cafeteria service.

This restaurant operates on a fiscal year basis ending on September 30 of each year. Many businesses use a fiscal rather than the calendar year, as they find it more convenient to get an accurate statement prepared at the time of the year when business is at a low ebb. The rush of New Year's Eve business is a big factor that might influence such a decision in many restaurants.

In this instance, the gross food cost is shown and no calculation is made for employees' meals. It may be of interest to compare the various cost and expense ratios of this restaurant with those covered by the other three exhibits. From them it is undoubtedly possible to gain some idea of the differences in operating policy as reflected in the cost ratios for the main elements of operation shown in these summaries. They also serve to show the adaptability of this form of statement to the wide variety of restaurants which make up the membership of the National Restaurant Association and, at the same time, the advantages that may accrue to the restaurant man when the Uniform System of Accounts for Restaurants is put to use.

Exhibit J is also an example of a restaurant corporation balance sheet and, in this case, the company owns the property in which it is doing business.

Exhibit I

SUMMARY PROFIT AND LOSS STATEMENT
A LARGE RESTAURANT—TABLE, COUNTER AND
CAFETERIA SERVICE FOOD ONLY
YEAR ENDED SEPTEMBER 30, 19

	Amounts	Percentages
FOOD SALES	$1,825,000	100.00%
COST OF FOOD SOLD	690,000	37.81
GROSS PROFIT	$1,135,000	62.19%
OTHER INCOME	8,500	.47
TOTAL INCOME	$1,143,500	62.66%
CONTROLLABLE EXPENSES		
Payroll	$ 650,000	35.62%
Payroll Taxes and Employee Benefits	65,500	3.59
Employees' meals	Not Figured	
Direct Operating Expenses	75,000	4.11
Advertising and Promotion	12,500	.69
Utilities	36,500	2.00
Administrative and General	46,000	2.52
Repairs and Maintenance	25,500	1.39
Total Controllable Expenses	$ 911,000	49.92%
PROFIT BEFORE RENT OR OCCUPATION COSTS	$ 232,500	12.74%
OCCUPATION COSTS—		
TAXES, INTEREST, INSURANCE, ETC.	65,000	3.56
PROFIT BEFORE DEPRECIATION	$ 167,500	9.18%
DEPRECIATION	30,600	1.68
NET PROFIT ON RESTAURANT OPERATIONS	$ 136,900	7.50%
DIVIDENDS RECEIVED	4,050	.22
TOTAL PROFIT BEFORE INCOME TAXES	$ 140,950	7.72%
FEDERAL INCOME TAX ESTIMATE	59,500	3.26
NET PROFIT TO EARNED SURPLUS	$ 81,450	4.46%

BALANCE SHEET
A LARGE RESTAURANT—TABLE,
COUNTER AND CAFETERIA SERVICE
AS AT SEPTEMBER 30, 19

ASSETS

CURRENT ASSETS
Cash
On Hand	$ 3,000		
On Deposit	56,250		
Total Cash		$ 59,250	
Accounts Receivable		2,700	

Inventories
Food	$ 16,750		
Candy, Tobacco, Novelties	12,250		
Supplies	2,500		
Total Inventories		31,500	
Marketable Securities		81,000	
(Market Value September 30 — $93,150)			
Prepaid Expenses		7,050	
Total Current Assets			$181,500

FIXED ASSETS
Land		$ 62,250	
Building	$445,000		
Deduct Depreciation Reserve	170,000	275,000	
Furniture, Fixtures and Equipment	$140,000		
Deduct Depreciation Reserve	85,000	55,000	
Air Conditioning and Refrigeration	$ 55,000		
Deduct Depreciation Reserve	33,000	22,000	
Automobiles	$ 7,850		
Deduct Depreciation Reserve	5,250	2,600	

Reserve Stock—Operating Equipment
China and Glassware	$ 7,550		
Linens	3,200		
Silverware	6,000		
Uniforms	1,250	18,000	
Total Fixed Assets			434,850
TOTAL ASSETS			$616,350

LIABILITIES AND CAPITAL

CURRENT LIABILITIES

Accounts Payable—Trade Creditors		$ 46,000	
Taxes Collected		13,200	
Accrued Expenses			
Payroll	$ 12,500		
Sales Taxes—State and City	4,550		
Utilities	2,500		
Social Security Taxes	2,150		
Interest on Mortgage	3,300		
Real Estate and Personal Property Taxes	12,250		
Compensation Insurance	1,800		
Total Accrued Expenses		39,050	
Federal Income Tax		59,500	
Current Mortgage Payments		12,000	
Total Current Liabilities			$169,750

FIRST MORTGAGE—6½ LOAN

FIRST MORTGAGE—6½ LOAN		$211,350	
Deduct Current Payment due Quarterly		12,000	
Balance—Noncurrent			199,350

CAPITAL AND RETAINED EARNINGS

Common Stock—1,500 Shares at $100 per Share		$150,000	
Retained Earnings			
Balance—October 1, 19	$ 60,800		
Profit—Year Ended September 30, 19	81,450		
Total	$142,250		
Dividends Paid	45,000		
Balance—September 30, 19		97,250	
Total Capital and Retained Earnings			247,250

TOTAL LIABILITIES AND CAPITAL	$616,350

EXHIBITS K AND L

Because of the growth of Drive-in Service Restaurants in the past ten years it was decided that example financial statements for this type of operation should be included in this book. Again, the adaptability and versatility of the Uniform System are illustrated in these examples, shown in Exhibits K and L.

The chain or multiple operation was purposely avoided in seeking these examples, which are based on a composite of several actual operations. This does not mean that chain operations cannot conform to the Uniform System, for many of them do. However, the elements of central office and commissary expenses require additional scheduled statements and the division of these expenses to the operating units is not deemed necessary for control or, more often, is made on a basis not readily comparable to other operations. Also, in many cases there is a combination of company owned and franchise operations which makes the division of central company expenses difficult or arbitrary.

In Exhibit K the expense items for direct operating expenses, advertising, administrative and general are shown in some detail to illustrate the relative amounts involved and the suggested category in which to place such items as auto expense, receipts deposit service, franchise fees, etc.

The corporation in the example leases the site on which the operating unit is located. Exhibit L shows loans from stockholders, made primarily to insure good credit standing with purveyors by prompt payment of current bills. You will also note a $790 deficiency in working capital, with current assets at $27,475 and current liabilities at $28,265. This is illustrative of the fact that in an operation of this sort, which is virtually on a cash basis, a one-to-one ratio is not an unusual condition.

PROFIT AND LOSS STATEMENT
A DRIVE-IN RESTAURANT YEAR ENDED DECEMBER 31, 19

		Amounts	Percentages
SALES		$350,000	100.00%
FOOD COST		130,000	37.14
GROSS PROFIT		$220,000	62.86%
CONTROLLABLE EXPENSES			
Payroll—Management	$18,000		
Staff	83,000	$101,000	28.86%
Payroll Taxes and Employee Benefits		7,000	2.00
Employees' Meals		2,500	.71
Direct Operating Expenses			
Paper Supplies	$13,000		
Cleaning Supplies	1,050		
Laundry	1,925		
Uniforms	1,050		
China, Glassware, Silver, Utensils	2,450		
Auto Expense	1,550		
Other	950	21,975	6.28
Advertising		6,650	1.90
Utilities		9,100	2.60
Administrative and General			
Office Expense	$ 2,025		
Dues and Subscriptions	150		
Insurance—General	1,150		
Cash Shortages	75		
Legal and Audit Fees	2,100		
Brink's Deposit Service	1,800		
Franchise Fees	6,125		
Miscellaneous	785	14,210	4.06
Repairs and Maintenance			
Building and Grounds	$ 4,250		
Equipment	3,200	7,450	2.13
Total Controllable Expenses		$169,885	48.54%
PROFIT BEFORE RENT, ETC.		$ 50,115	14.32%
RENT OR OCCUPATION COSTS			
Ground Rent		$ 7,200	2.06%
Real Estate and Personal Property Taxes		4,200	1.20
Sewer Tax		600	.17
Insurance on Property		2,500	.72
Interest on Loans		1,200	.34
Total Rent or Occupation Costs		$ 15,700	4.49%
PROFIT BEFORE DEPRECIATION		$ 34,415	9.83%
DEPRECIATION		12,750	3.64
PROFIT BEFORE INCOME TAXES		$ 21,665	6.19%
FEDERAL INCOME TAX		4,765	1.36
NET PROFIT		$ 16,900	4.83%

Exhibit L

BALANCE SHEET

A DRIVE-IN RESTAURANT
AS AT DECEMBER 31, 19--

ASSETS

CURRENT ASSETS
Change Funds	$ 900		
Cash on Deposit	18,350		
Total Cash		$ 19,250	
Advances to Employees		350	
Inventories—Food	$ 1,850		
Supplies	1,200		
Total Inventories		3,050	
Deposits—Utilities	$ 825		
Rent	600		
Total Deposits		1,425	
Prepaid Expenses		3,400	
Total Current Assets			$ 27,475

	Cost	Depreciation Reserve	
FIXED ASSETS			
Building	$ 75,000	$ 37,500	
Leasehold Improvements	30,000	18,000	
Furnishings and Equipment	66,900	40,140	
Sign	6,000	3,600	
Automobiles	5,225	1,750	
Total Fixed Assets	$183,125	$100,990	82,135
TOTAL ASSETS			$109,610

LIABILITIES AND CAPITAL INVESTMENT

CURRENT LIABILITIES
Accounts Payable—Trade Creditors	$ 12,500	
Taxes Collected	3,875	
Accrued Expenses	6,800	
Accrued Federal Income Tax	4,765	
Unclaimed Wages and Key Deposits	325	
Total Current Liabilities		$ 28,265
LOANS—FROM STOCKHOLDERS—6%		15,500
CAPITAL STOCK AND RETAINED EARNINGS		
Capital Stock	$ 30,000	
Retained Earnings (Surplus)	35,845	
Total Capital		65,845
TOTAL LIABILITIES AND CAPITAL		$109,610

EXHIBIT M

With the permission of the American Hotel Association and the Club Managers' Association of America, Exhibit M is presented here to show the form recommended in their respective Uniform Systems for the food and beverage departmental operations in hotels and clubs. It happens that these forms are almost identical.

Because the food and beverage operation is only one of several departments, a hotel or club can obtain uniformity and exactness in their statement presentation only to the extent of the direct costs and expenses of that department. This means that the departmental payroll cost comprises only the service, kitchen, warewashing, storeroom, checkers and cashiers, and that salaries and wages of the management and auditing office, engine room and maintenance crews are charged to overhead or to unapportioned expenses. Also their expenses consist only of the direct operating expenses and such items as advertising and promotion, utilities, administrative and general, repairs and maintenance, and the fixed charges for rent, etc., are not included in this departmental statement.

Thus, the hotel or club could not achieve the same comparative uniformity as is suggested for restaurant operations due to the multiple income producing departments such as rooms, restaurant, telephone, laundry and valet, cigar stand, etc., all of which contribute their departmental profits to cover the overhead expenses and fixed charges mentioned in the previous paragraph. This same circumstance may be true of an in-plant feeding operation, a department store restaurant, or an institution, since in these instances the feeding operation is only a part of the entire operation, and it is difficult to apportion all of the expenses to it. As previously stated, there is the further difficulty that in many instances the accounting statements must conform to the requirements of an entire institution, and this becomes more important than achieving uniformity with other types of feeding operations.

Hotels and clubs also use a form of statement for their food and beverage operations which divides all of the costs and expenses and arrives at a separate departmental operating result for each of these major types of sales.

Some restaurant operators have also found this form to be desirable, but here again the division of many of the expenses, in order to arrive at a net profit for food and one for beverage, requires a formula often based on an arbitrary division dictated by individual desires and experience, and it is not possible to obtain uniformity in statement presentation on this basis.

For this reason, the Uniform System of Accounts for Restaurants attempts no such division and leaves the individual restaurant man to work it out according to his own dictates and desires. The classification of accounts will not be changed by any such procedure and most restaurants use the combined form outlined in this book.

FOOD AND BEVERAGE DEPARTMENTAL OPERATIONS
ACCORDING TO UNIFORM SYSTEM OF ACCOUNTS
FOR HOTELS AND CLUBS

	Combined Total	Food	Beverages
GROSS SALES			
Dining Rooms (List Each Room)	$	$	$
Room Service			
Banquets			
Total Gross Sales	$	$	$
ALLOWANCES			
NET SALES	$	$	$
COST OF SALES			
Cost of Supplies Consumed	$	$	$
Less Cost of Employees' Meals			
Cost of Sales	$	$	$
GROSS PROFIT	$	$	$
OTHER INCOME			
Cover Charges			
Sundry Banquet Income and Miscellaneous			
TOTAL REVENUE	$	$	$
DEPARTMENTAL EXPENSES			
Salaries and Wages	$	$	$
Vacation Pay (Hotel's Only)			
Employees' Meals			
Employee Relations (Hotel's Only)			
Uniforms			
Music and Entertainment			
Laundry			
Kitchen Fuel			
Linen			
China and Glassware			
Silver			
Utensils			
Cleaning Supplies			
Dry Cleaning			
Contract Cleaning			
Guest Supplies			
Paper Supplies			
Menus and Beverage Lists			
Printing and Stationery			
Decorations			
Banquet Expenses			
Cost Accounting			
Licenses and Taxes			
Bar Expenses			
Wine Cellar Expense			
Miscellaneous			
Total Expenses	$	$	$
DEPARTMENTAL PROFIT (OR LOSS)	$	$	$

NOTE: You will note that this form of statement uses only first 5 categories in uniform system of accounts for restaurants and only direct payroll for service, kitchen, sanitation and bar.

RECORD KEEPING
FOR THE
SMALL RESTAURANT

PART III

RECORD KEEPING FOR THE SMALL RESTAURANT

Although the suggested forms contained in this section are intended for the small operator and the text is addressed to him, we felt that they should, at the same time, be complete enough to illustrate how they can be outlined to give the individual proprietor the same complete picture of his business and the same amount of help from his statements that is enjoyed by the larger restaurants who have a full time bookkeeper. For this reason the forms illustrated may in some instances be more detailed than is necessary, in which case the restaurant operator will use only those columns and spaces to fit his individual needs.

In order to avoid confusing the small operator no attempt is made in this text to explain any technical accounting points, such as the difference between the cash basis or accrual basis of accounting, the use of prepaid or accrued expenses, depreciation reserves, or the like. In the event the proprietor or manager is not familiar with bookkeeping methods we suggest that a part-time bookkeeper may be employed to make the necessary closing entries each month and to prepare the profit and loss statement and balance sheet.

A profit and loss statement is a summary, in dollars and cents, of the operating transactions of a restaurant which are made during the period of time it covers. To correctly reflect the financial results of operation in the restaurant business, as in any other, certain adjustments must be made to the accumulated daily figures compiled during the month by the proprietor or his bookkeeper. These adjustments will include the changes in the value of food, beverage, and other inventories carried as between the beginning and end of the accounting period, assuming that regular inventories are taken for control purposes and that their fluctuations are sufficient to affect the food cost and other costs where the amount of goods on hand is a factor. The adjustments will also include a charge to operations to cover the depreciation on the furniture and equipment and on the building if it is part of the invest-ment in the business and the amortization of the leasehold value and lease-hold improvements made. These depreciations charges are an operating expense of the business, the amount of which is usually determined by a calculation or estimate of the useful life of the property. Some of the other expenses, such as insurance, taxes, and licenses, are paid on an annual basis and it may be desirable to apportion them over the period of the monthly statements by an adjustment which would result in charging one-twelfth to the operating costs of the current month. These and other similar items are adjustments which require experience with double-entry bookkeeping, and which may be left to the part-time bookkeeper or accountant to handle at the end of the month or period.

Thus, it is obvious that, unless statements are prepared purely on a cash receipts and disbursements basis, someone with a knowledge of double-entry bookkeeping will be required to prepare them properly. It is also obvious that this book cannot be a bookkeeping text. The primary purpose for which this section was prepared was to illustrate how the smaller restaurant opera-tors can aid themselves by a good record of daily transactions and be in a position to have proper statements with a minimum of work on the part of a bookkeeper or accountant at the end of the month or at the time of the yearly statement and tax return.

Business is conducted for profit and consequently the question arises— "How much did I make or lose?" This is followed by the natural question of, "Is my plan of operation working out successfully?" These are questions that the profit and loss statement will answer and it will serve as a guide that a simple but adequate bookkeeping system will make possible. The extent of the answers to questions on sales, food costs, other expenses, and profits depends, of course, on the amount of detail the records make available.

As previously stated, the object of the forms outlined in this section is primarily to place the proprietor in a position, with only a few entries each day, to have the records necessary to accumulate the daily transactions in a manner that will facilitate preparation of a monthly statement. Thus, all of the instructions in connection with these forms are directed toward the daily use of the sample forms by the proprietor or someone he selects. If the entries are made daily, correct record keeping will not be a burden or nuisance, and the proprietor can easily keep abreast of his business as it progresses.

It is also the intention of this section to free the minds of the proprietor of a small restaurant from the thought that "bookkeeping and bookkeepers" are a necessary nuisance who continually annoy them with detail and thereby make them fight figures, and instead to implant the idea that properly compiled figures can become an invaluable tool to be used in improving the situation through the knowledge that can be gained from them.

That is why the earlier statement was made of the fact that the bookkeeping forms, as outlined, were designed to give complete detail on operations if desired, but also are flexible enough so that the user could eliminate any detail in which he is not interested and retain only that part which is practical in his case.

The Daily Report—Form No. 4 is a case in point. The operator of a simple small restaurant serving food only and interested purely in daily cash sales will not need to go to the bother of using this form, but can make the daily entries directly on Form No. 1—Sales and Cash Receipts. However, Form No. 4 has been included to demonstrate how a proprietor who is interested in obtaining the information on the sales by meals, the customer count, and the average sale per customer, can prepare a daily record of this type, to be transcribed to Form No. 1 for the purpose of compiling the monthly totals. We strongly recommend that, if possible, a record of sales by meals and the customer count be kept as an additional tool for management in facilitating its analysis or the reasons for fluctuations in expenses and changes in net profit.

The forms suggested for daily use in a small restaurant are as follows:

Form No. 1—SALES AND CASH RECEIPTS

Form No. 2—CASH DISBURSEMENTS

Form No. 3—RECORD OF UNPAID BILLS

Form No. 5—WEEKLY PAYROLL SHEET

Form No. 6—EMPLOYMENT CARD

The use of Daily Report Form No. 4 is optional, as stated earlier, but if it is not used we advise the use of a memorandum book in which to record the daily "Cash Paid Out Of Drawer." The totals from this memorandum book can then be summarized and entered in the "Cash Disbursements" form at the end of the month.

At the close of the month the proprietor or part-time bookkeeper will need a Journal and a General Ledger for the monthly closing, and the accumulation of the figures for the profit and loss statement and the balance sheet. If the daily work is kept up to date, a bookkeeper need spend only a few hours at the end of the month, and it should be fairly easy to find someone to do this work on a part-time basis.

For convenience, the money columns in each form are numbered so that they can be more easily understood by a person not trained in bookkeeping methods. As previously stated, this book makes no attempt to teach bookkeeping or accounting. Therefore, the text has been kept free of technical terms and the main concern has been with the daily transactions.

SALES AND CASH RECEIPTS—FORM NO. 1

The permanent record of cash receipts might be a simple cash book in which each day's receipts are recorded or, if the operator wishes to separate cash sales from cash received from other sources, two account columns and a descriptive column could be used. However, if it seems desirable to segregate sales into various categories, such as food, beverages, cigar stand, etc., and the restaurant has receipts from other sources as well as the complication of charge sales, a book or sheets with sufficient columns is recommended to cover each group of transactions as outlined in Form No. 1.

The latter is the intention of Form No. 1 illustrated in this text which the operator of a small restaurant will find convenient. It is possible and practical, of course, to use any columnar book or set of ruled sheets, such as are obtained in any local stationery store, by heading up the columns as suggested herein or as they may be changed to suit individual needs.

The purpose of this Sales and Cash Receipts Form is to accumulate the daily sales and cash receipts in their proper categories so that the columns will show the monthly total of each type of receipt, the total charges and collections on customer's accounts, and the total cash deposited in that period. The following headings are used:

DATE—It is mandatory to use a separate line for each day's transactions, and more than one line may be used, if necessary, to describe the transactions for the day properly.

		Amount Columns
Credits	Food Sales	1
	Beverage Sales	2
	Cigar Counter Sales	3
	Sales Taxes	4
	Tips Charged	5
	Customers' Accounts Collected	6
	Miscellaneous Receipts	7
	Cash over and (short)	8
TOTAL SALES AND RECEIPTS		9
Debits	Cash Paid Out of Drawer	
	Tips Paid	10
	Other Payments	11
	Customers Accounts Charged	12
	Bank Deposit	13

In a very small operation the proprietor may not want to go to the trouble of dividing the sales as to food, beverages, and cigar stand and other items. In this case, it is quite probable that the cash receipts will represent the sales for the day. Also in this case, there may be occasional items representing cash received, such as advances of additional capital investment, repayment of loans made to employees or others, sales of old equipment, etc., and these items should be shown separately under, "Miscellaneous Receipts." Thus only Columns (1) and (7) are used to record sales and other receipts; Column

(11) for petty cash payments made for purchases or services; Column (9) for total sales and receipts and Column (13) for the bank deposit. The record for this small operation would use only 5 of the 13 columns shown in Form No. 1, as indicated in the following example:

Date

Column 1	Food Sales		$100.00
Column 7	Miscellaneous Receipts		
	Telephone Commissions	$ 5.50	
	Loan Repaid	10.00	15.50
Column 9	Total Receipts		$115.50
Column 11	Cash Paid Out of Drawer		
	Groceries—Food Cost	4.20	
	Cleaning Supplies	.95	5.15
Column 13	Bank Deposit		$110.35

If a cash register is used it is possible to separate the sales as to breakfast, lunch, dinner, etc., by reading the register at the end of each meal period. If guest checks are used they can be used in making this division as well as that between food, beverages, cigar stand sales, taxes and tips charged. Guest checks also facilitate the compilation of a count of the number of customers served although some registers are also designed to give the number of customers as well as the money totals. Thus, both register and guests checks can be used to amplify the daily accumulation of information on sales as well as to serve their primary function, which is the internal control on sales.

DATE COLUMN

As a rule only one line on the form will be required for each day, but more may be used if necessary. For instance, it may be necessary to use two or more lines to describe miscellaneous receipts.

COLUMN 1—FOOD SALES

Enter the total food sales for the day in this column.

COLUMN 2—BEVERAGE SALES

If liquor, beer or wine is sold it is highly advisable to separate these sales from the food sales. The manner of separation is not covered here inasmuch as it is assumed that if the volume of these sales is sufficient to warrant separation the means to do so will also be present, either by cash register, guest checks, or otherwise.

In the event, beverage sales will include soft drinks, but no coffee, tea or milk, which are included in food sales.

Separate columns will be necessary for each category of beverage sales if this is desirable. This may be accomplished by lengthening the sales portion of this form or by keeping a subsidiary record that ties in with Column 2.

COLUMN 3—CIGAR COUNTER

Many restaurants have a counter at the cashier's stand for the sale of cigars, cigarettes, candy, gum and other items. It is advisable to show these sales separately from food and beverage sales and a separate column is provided on this form to record them.

COLUMN 4 — SALES TAXES

In many states and municipalities sales taxes are collected from the customer and are accounted for separately, and for this reason a separate column is provided for the taxes that are a part of daily sales.

If tax collections are kept separately, the total will be credited to a sales tax account in the general ledger and amounts paid to the government will be charged to this same clearing account.

Smaller restaurants, and some of the larger ones, often find it more practical to include these sales tax collections with sales and to charge the payments to the government to "administrative and general expense." Although in exact accounting the inclusion of sales taxes in the sales may affect the food cost and expense ratios, it is a matter of judgment and practical application whether the distortion is significant enough to warrant a separate accounting for these taxes collected.

CREDIT EXTENSION AND TIPS CHARGED

Restaurants are feeling the pressure of the demand for credit accounts, and this type of sale has expanded widely in all lines of retail and consumer sales in the past few years. The tremendous growth in popularity of the many credit card agencies is good evidence of this trend.

Although sales of most smaller restaurants are on a cash basis, there has been a trend toward some charge sales and for that reason Form No. 1 includes one column (12) for the recording of the charge sales for the day and one column (6), for recording the collections on charge sales previously made. It is advisable, in the event the proprietor adopts the policy of extending credit to his customers, that the details of these transactions should be noted in a separate book or record.

The details of the charges and collections on charge accounts can then be totaled daily for entry in the Sales and Cash Receipts Record — Form No. 1.

An example of this type of record is included on the reverse side of the Daily Report — Form No. 4, included as an exhibit later in this section. The record should at least include the date, the amount charged and the customer's name. In a small restaurant it may not be necessary to send out bills for the few charges made, but in the event it is necessary to do so there should be a record of the customer's address and credit card number, if any.

The policy of allowing the customer to obtain meals on credit by signing his check also poses the problem of what to do when he adds the amount of a tip to the check, which has become the prevailing procedure. Usually these tips are paid out of the cash drawer to the waiter or waitress, who signs a tip voucher as a receipt. This also makes it necessary in the daily records to provide separate columns in which to record the amount of tips charged and the tips paid. Form No. 1, therefore, provides columns (5) and (10), respectively, for this purpose. These two columns should balance daily unless one of the servers forgets to collect. Since the cashier will ordinarily keep all charge checks separate from the cash sales, the total amount of tips charged can be transcribed from them as the charges are listed. In many of the larger restaurants the cashier's sheets provide the data for compiling these records.

COLUMN 5 — TIPS CHARGED

The daily total of all tips added to charge checks by customers will be recorded in this column. The total of this column will be credited to a clearing account in the general books, offset by the total of the tips paid, Column (10).

COLUMN 6 — COLLECTED ACCOUNTS

In this column the daily total of all collections from customers' charges that were made on prior days is recorded. These collections are not a part of today's sales and for that reason the cash received must be shown separately in order to keep the correct sales totals.

COLUMN 7 — MISCELLANEOUS RECEIPTS

Enter in this column the sales of items other than food, beverages, or cigar stand. Such other miscellaneous income items as commissions from vending machines, waste paper and bottle sales, sub-rentals, etc., are entered here. Also enter in this column any cash receipts that are not ordinarily rung up on the cash register, such as additional investments of the proprietor, loans, sales of equipment, etc. An explanation column is provided for a description of each such item and a separate line can be used for each, if there are more than one on a particular day.

COLUMN 8 — CASH OVER OR (SHORT)

If cash registers or guest checks are used to account for sales, it may be that the cash turned in by the cashier for deposit may be over or short of the amounts shown in the registers or on guest checks. The amount of this difference will be shown in Column (8), written clearly in black ink if the cash is "over" or greater than the sales figure, or written in parentheses or in red ink if it is "short" of, or less than the sales figure.

COLUMN 9 — DAILY TOTALS

The first eight columns are added and the total is placed in Column (9), which shows the sales and cash receipts to be accounted for on that day. The first eight columns are all recorded in the credit side of the general ledger.

The total of Columns (10), (11) and (12) also equal the amount shown in Column (9) and in this manner the transactions are kept in balance. This is the principle of what is called "double entry bookkeeping" and the fact that both sets of columns equal the total column will assure the proprietor that his recorded receipts are accounted for correctly.

COLUMNS 10 AND 11 — CASH PAID OUT OF DRAWER

The amounts entered in these columns are the petty cash payments made from the cash on hand at the restaurant. Column (10) is for the tips paid out on charge checks, the total of which should offset the amount shown in Column (5). Column (11) is for payments made for supplies and services out of the cashier's funds, which are explained in the adjacent column provided.

Any amounts withheld as fees charged by any credit card or collection agency on any remittance in payment of customers charges should be recorded in this explanatory column in order that the customer's account will receive full credit in Column (6) for payments made on his account. Thus, Column (11) will cover both petty cash payments out of the drawer and these retained fees, and it is advisable to show each type of transaction separately.

It is very likely, except in the very small restaurant, that the number of petty cash transactions will require more than one line. Therefore, it would be advisable and practical to keep a small memorandum book at the cashier's stand in which the individual payments are recorded and added. Each day's total may then be entered from this memorandum book in Column (11).

The sample entries shown in Form No. 1 for Column (11) indicate the type of petty cash transactions that might be involved. At the bottom of this column, after the total for the month is recorded, a summary of the transactions should be made for posting to the general books.

COLUMN 12 – CUSTOMERS ACCOUNTS CHARGED

The total of all charge sales to customers for the day will be recorded in this column. These charges are a part of today's sales and for that reason their amount must be deducted from the sales in order to arrive at the net cash receipts.

COLUMN 13 – BANK DEPOSITS

Many small restaurant operators keep all of their funds in cash in a safe in the restaurant or take it home each night, and all of their payments are made in cash. Neither practice is wise either from the standpoint of safety or of keeping personal and business transactions separate. If personal cash and business cash is intermingled, it may be very difficult to balance the records of, or prepare an accurate statement on the business. The best way to make this separation is to open a separate checking account for the business. It is also advisable that each day's receipts be deposited intact and that all disbursements be made by check. In doing this there will automatically be a record which will be invaluable in keeping the accounts in order and serving as a double check on their accuracy by means of the monthly bank statement. In addition, the bank provides a safe place for funds on hand. In the event a receipt is lost, the cancelled bank check can take its place as evidence of the expenditure for income tax or other purposes.

In the event several days' receipts are deposited at one time it is advisable to make separate deposits for each day in order that the bank deposits can easily be traced to the restaurant records.

Column (13), which is the total of all sales and other cash receipts minus the petty cash payments and charge sales made that day, represents the net cash taken in that day, which is the amount to be deposited in the bank.

The following example, based on the figures taken from the sample transactions of April 3, shown in Form No. 1, will illustrate how to arrive at the amount to be deposited.

Total Sales and Receipts—Columns 1 to 8		$770.95
Deduct:		
Cash paid out of drawer		
Tips—Column 10	$ 5.00	
Other—Column 11	2.25	
Charge Sales—Column 12	32.80	40.05
Bank Deposit—Column 13		$730.90

SALES AND CASH RECEIPTS
FOR MONTH OF _April_ 19___

FORM 1

	CREDITS										DEBITS			
	1	2	3	4	5	6	MIS'C'L. RECEIPTS		8	9	CASH OUT OF DRAWER		12	13
DATE	FOOD SALES	BEVERAGE SALES	CIGAR COUNTER	SALES TAXES	TIPS CHARGED	CUSTOMERS' ACCOUNTS COLLECTED	7 AMOUNT	EXPLANATION	CASH OVER OR (SHORT)	DAILY TOTALS	10 TIPS PAID	11 OTHER PAYMENTS / EXPLANATION	CUSTOMERS' ACCOUNTS CHARGED	BANK DEPOSIT
April 1	657.45	163.50	15.30	25.10					(5.15)	856.20		12.00 beverages		844.20
2	621.15	159.80	15.65	23.65		15.20	350.00 unusual/additional		5.00	433.45		5.50 food		433.25
3	576.60	143.25	14.00	22.00	5.00	4.65	6.00 W. Bell		(.55)	770.95	5.00	2.25 food	32.10	732.90
4	412.35	140.20	12.50	19.00	3.00	12.80				669.65	3.00		20.40	646.45
5	620.25	151.50	16.65	23.65			45.00 juke box		(.65)	856.40		6.20 cleaning / 5.00 advertising		845.20
6	(Sunday — closed)													
7	634.30	162.35	14.65	24.35					.65	836.50		5.65 stationery		830.85
8	596.60	147.10	13.	19.70					.80	677.55				677.55
⋮														
29														
30	562.40	155.50	15.35	22.60		10.30			(1.65)	765.00		6.65 beverages		778.15
31														
TOTALS	16,000.00	4,000.00	460.00	612.00	26.50	150.00	363.00		(100.00)	21,085.50	26.50	130.00	185.00	21,467.00

Recapitulation
of Mis'c'l. Receipts
3,500.00 Bank Loan
6.00 Tel. Commission
10.00 Coin Machine
240.00 Beverage Sales
_____
3,630.00 Total

Recapitulation
of Other Payments
25.00 Stationery
22.00 Advertising
15.42 Cleaning Supplies
42.12 Food Purchases
25.46 Beverage Purchases
_____
130.00 Total

CASH DISBURSEMENTS—FORM NO. 2

Although we believe the form illustrated in this text to be a convenient one for the small restaurant operator, as in the case of Form No. 1, a columnar book or set of sheets may be used to serve the purpose by merely heading up the various columns as suggested or as they may be changed to suit individual needs.

The record of cash disbursements shown on Form No. 2 is really a check record and a purchase journal, combined for simplicity and for the convenience of the operator of a small restaurant. The primary purpose of the form is to provide for the recording of all checks drawn and classifying the expenditures for statement purposes.

The checks should be entered in numerical order as they are drawn and each given a separate line. It is advisable to enter each check on the day it is made out. This keeps the record up to date, so that at the end of the month it need only be totaled for posting to the general ledger.

The first three columns, which are not numbered, are for the date of the check, the name of payee and the check number, all of which are self explanatory. As in Form No. 1, the money columns have been numbered for convenient reference.

COLUMN 1—AMOUNT OF CHECK

Enter here the exact amount of each check drawn.

COLUMN 2—TAXES WITHHELD

In some of the smaller restaurants the payroll is paid in cash and a separate memorandum book is kept of the payroll detail. In some of the larger restaurants a separate payroll bank account is used, the total amount of the payroll being transferred from the general bank account for this purpose each pay-day and separate payroll records are kept to show the detail for each employee.

A weekly payroll Form No. 5 has been added to this section, which form is designed to provide a means for keeping such tax and other payroll elements properly entered. This form will facilitate proper recording and will also denote compliance with the federal and state Wage and Hour Regulations.

Where there are only a few employees, possibly ten to twenty, their checks can be drawn on the regular bank account and entered in detail on the cash disbursements record.

The Weekly Payroll Sheet—Form No. 5, described later in this section, indicates how total payroll, employee deductions and net payroll are to be entered in the Cash Disbursements—Form No. 2. By entering the cash on "take home" pay in Column (1), the payroll deductions in Column (2) and the employees' cash advances in Column (11), you will note that the amounts equal the total payroll cost which will be recorded in Column (8).

Some employers also arrange for their employees to purchase U.S. Bonds on a payroll plan and others have a pension or group insurance plan to which the employees contribute. These deductions can also be shown in Column (2). For convenience in keeping track of the various items withheld it is advisable to denote each item with a symbol, "W" for withholding, "O" for old age benefit, "B" for U.S. Bonds and "I" for insurance, etc. Then, after Column (2) is totaled, a recapitulation showing each item can be noted below the total for the convenience of the bookkeeper in posting to the general ledger.

The total of this column denotes the liability of the business to the government and others for payroll taxes, etc., withheld, for in this case the restaurant operator is acting as a collection agent.

COLUMN 3—DISCOUNTS

In many cases a purveyor may allow a discount for bills paid within 10 days or within a month. These discounts represent earnings to the restaurant operator and should be included with "other income" on the operating statement. For this reason Column (3) has been provided to record the savings due to prompt payment.

Many small operators do not bother to enter the discounts, feeling that the amounts are too small to warrant accounting for them. In that case the total and the distribution columns also show the net amount of the check issued in payment of their bills.

COLUMN 4—TOTAL

The first three columns are added and the total is placed in Column (4), denoting the amount that is to be charged to the distribution columns. The first three columns are all recorded on the credit side of the general ledger.

You will note that Columns (5) to (11) also equal this same total and that in this manner the transactions are kept in balance. As previously stated under the section, "Form No. 1," this is the principle of "double entry bookkeeping" and the fact that both sets of columns equal the total column indicates that the proprietor has made distribution of all of the disbursements.

COLUMN 5—ACCOUNTS PAYABLE

Just as provision was made in the Sales and Cash Receipts—Form No. 1 for charge sales to be recorded as income on the day the sale is made even though the amount is collected at a later date, some provision must also be made for expenses and other liabilities incurred during the current operating period but which are paid by the restaurant at a later date. Such expenses result in an account payable and should be recorded in the month or period to which they apply. For this reason, Record Of Unpaid Bills—Form No. 3 has been included in this section, and it will be described later in this text.

If Form No. 3 is used or if by some similar method a bill or liability has already been recorded on the books in a prior period, the payment of this item will be entered in Column (5)—Accounts Payable. If it should happen that a bill which applies to a prior period has not already been entered as an account payable, it will, of course, not be entered in Column (5) but will be treated as a cost or expense for the current month.

COLUMNS 5 TO 11

Columns (5) to (11) are used to show the nature and distribution of the expenditures made during the month. Because of the number of expense accounts in the profit and loss statement, it is convenient to group them under

108

main headings, such as food and beverage purchases, payroll, employee relations, other controllable expenses and other expenditures. In Part I of this book devoted to the Uniform System of Accounts for Restaurants there is a full explanation of how these totals fit into the preparation of the operating statement and balance sheet and of the proper column in which to enter each expenditure.

COLUMN 6 — FOOD

Enter in Column (6) all payments for food purchases which have not already been entered on Form No. 3 in prior periods. Also enter here the charge for delivery of foodstuffs, freight, express and cartage.

COLUMN 7 — BEVERAGES

If the restaurant includes a bar or cocktail lounge a separate account should be kept of the beverage costs. Therefore, Column (7) provides for the entry of all payments for beverage purchases which have not already been entered in Form No. 3 in prior periods.

If the restaurant does not operate a bar or cocktail lounge it may be found convenient to use this column for recording the purchases of cigar stand items. In a small restaurant the purchases of cigars, cigarettes, candy, etc., are infrequent enough so that it would be practical to enter them in Column (11) — "Other Disbursements" placing a proper symbol or explanation opposite each such entry.

COLUMN 8 — PAYROLL

Enter in this column the amount of all salaries and wages paid. This amount should represent the actual payroll expense of the restaurant and will include not only the "take home" wages shown in Column (1) but also any taxes withheld shown in Column (2), which would be the total for payroll as recorded in Column (4). Do not enter the proprietor's drawings here as his earnings come from profits of the business and are not generally considered as a payroll expense.

If a payroll book is used it may be found practical to enter only the total of the payroll as shown in this record. This treatment holds true if a check is drawn to reimburse the payroll bank account, providing one is maintained.

If part of a payroll applies to a prior or succeeding month, the bookkeeper should make an entry in his journal at the end of the month applying the proper amount to each period for statement purposes. The small restaurant operator can disregard this complication of prepayments and accruals for all practical purposes since, for the most part, his payrolls are usually on a weekly basis and the amounts involved will not create any great distortion of the operating result between accounting periods. The subject is mentioned here only to indicate to those familiar with bookkeeping methods that such accruals may be necessary for complete accuracy in recording the payroll expense of each period. The small operator who does not wish to bother with accruals and whose weekly payroll has two or three days to run into the following month, should not total his cash disbursements record until that payroll has been entered.

109

COLUMN 9—EMPLOYEE BENEFITS

Payroll taxes and fringe benefits have become an important part of the expense of operating any business in the past few years and since these costs have a direct relation to the payroll they are, in effect, a part of the labor cost. To properly account for these expenses it is advisable to show them separately in the operating statement right next to the cash payroll, so that the proprietor can have a better picture of his total labor costs.

Enter in this column the payment of the restaurant's portion of Old Age Benefit Tax, Federal Unemployment Tax, State Unemployment Tax, Workmen's Compensation Insurance Premiums and any other fringe benefits the employees may receive as is outlined under the heading "Employee Benefits" in the Uniform System Of Accounts For Restaurants—Part I of this book.

COLUMN 10—OTHER CONTROLLABLE EXPENSES

Enter in this column all amounts paid for items included under this heading in the Uniform System of Accounts for Restaurants in Part I of this text. These include direct operating expenses, music and entertainment, advertising and promotion, utilities, administrative and general expenses and repairs and maintenance. For convenience, an explanation space is provided next to this column so that the exact nature of the item entered can be shown. These, in turn, may be summarized at the bottom of the column after it is totaled in order to facilitate a more detailed analysis of these expenses.

Any payment of items shown under "Rent and Occupational Costs" in Part I of the text and dealt with in the following comments on Column (11) should not be entered here.

COLUMN 11—OTHER DISBURSEMENTS

In a small restaurant the charges for rent or occupation costs are usually infrequent, so they will not require a separate column. For that reason we advise that these items, which include rent, fire and extended coverage insurance on the premises, interest paid, etc., be entered in Column (11) and a proper explanation given in the space provided.

All bills or payments not included in Columns (5) to (10) should also be entered in this column, and proper explanation given. Some of the items that would be entered in this column are: proprietor's drawings, payments on notes, contracts or loans, advances to employees, purchases of furniture or equipment, and the like.

GENERAL

By the use of the forms shown in this section the restaurant proprietor will be in a position to have a statement prepared showing his sales and other income, food and beverage costs, payroll and employee benefits, other controllable expenses, and rent or occupation costs. A knowledge of these major factors is essential to good operation.

The forms are prepared so that the information they compile can be expanded to the extent found convenient in each instance to meet the desire for more detail.

CASH DISBURSEMENTS

For Month of April 19_

DATE	NAME OF PAYEE	CHECK NUMBER	CREDITS — AMOUNT OF CHECK (1)	TAXES WITH-HELD (2)	DIS-COUNTS (3)	TOTAL (4)	ACCOUNTS PAYABLE (5)	FOOD (6)	BEVERAGE (7)	PAYROLL (8)	EMPLOYEE BENEFITS (9)	OTHER CONTROLLABLE EXPENSES AMOUNT (10)	EXPLANATION	OTHER DISBURSEMENTS AMOUNT (11)	EXPLANATION
2	Watson Meat Supply	332	212 42			212 42	212 42								
	First National Bank	333	91 25			91 25								91 25	5¼% interest on loan
	Chicago Real Estate Co.	334	500 00			500 00								500 00	rent April
	Yummy Baking	335	120 00			120 00	120 00								
	Easy Laundry	336	57 50			57 50	57 50								
3	Natl Supply Company	337	1250 00			1250 00	1250 00								
	Lowell Poultry Company	338	16 40			16 40	16 40								
	Farmers Produce	339	318 62			318 62	318 62								
	Equipment Mfg Company	340	38 76		40	39 16						39 16	utensils		
5	Payroll - week ending 4/5	341	2212 08	1712 92 / 575 00		2960 00				3000 00				100 00	Tips.
	Acme Supply Company	342	200 00			200 00	200 00							(120 00)	Insurance
	Widget Company	343	50 00			50 00			50 00					(20 00)	Advances
6	Smith Purveyor Company	344	72 00			72 00		72 00							
	TOTAL CHECKS DRAWN		22497 58	2058 00	37 30	24593 38	8570 00	4750 00	1250 00	6000 00	285 00	1130 00		2668 38	

178.48 Utilities
266.52 Adm & Gen.
155.00 Repairs
68.00 Advertising
362.00 Fixed Exp.
1130.00 Total

91.25 Interest
500.00 Rent
300.00 Kitchen Equip.
400.00 Repr. Assn.
1417.13 With. for Unpaid
(120.00) Insurance
(20.00) Advances
2668.38 Total

111

RECORD OF UNPAID BILLS—FORM NO. 3

At the end of the month or accounting period there are always some unpaid bills for goods or services that were received, but which have not been included in the expense classifications for that month. For this reason Form No. 3—Record Of Unpaid Bills has been devised as a means of entering them in the records and reflecting these expenses in their proper accounting period in the operating statements.

Through the Cash Disbursements—Form No. 2, all of the costs, expenses, and other accounts are charged for items that have been paid in the period, but the costs are not complete unless the items incurred and unpaid at the end of the period are also entered in the books.

The columns in Form No. 3 are similar to those on the Cash Disbursements—Form No. 2 and thus, it is not necessary to repeat their explanation here other than to advise that this form provides for the distribution of these unpaid items to their proper category and thus Columns (2) to (5) should equal Column (1). Because of the similarity of Forms No. 2 and No. 3, it is also possible to use a separate sheet of Form No. 2 for recording unpaid bills by a proper use of the columns.

It is assumed that accrued or prepaid payroll will be accounted for by the bookkeeper as previously explained in connection with Column (8)—Form No. 2, and this form makes no special provision for unpaid payroll. If it is found desirable to enter unpaid payroll here the distribution can be explained in Column (5).

The only column that needs an explanation here is the one entitled, "Date Paid." Usually, in a small operation the proprietor attempts to stay on a cash basis if possible. Thus, when a payment of one of the bills entered on this form is made in the following month or period it is well to refer to the sheet on which that unpaid bill is listed and to insert in the "Date Paid" column the date on which this bill is paid. This will provide for a continuous day-to-day record of unpaid bills, which will be the ones remaining without any date paid notation opposite them.

In cases where bills are allowed to remain unpaid for more than a month, or where part-payments are made, it might be found advisable to have the bookkeeper set up an accounts payable ledger. Ordinarily, in a small operation, this should not be necessary and the open items on Form No. 3 can be totaled to show the accounts payable.

RECORD OF UNPAID BILLS

FOR MONTH OF _April_ 19___

NAME OF CREDITOR	CREDIT AMOUNT OF BILL 1	DATE PAID	DEBITS						
			FOOD 2	BEVERAGE 3	CONTROLLABLE EXPENSES AMOUNT 4	EXPLANATION	OTHER ITEMS AMOUNT 5	EXPLANATION	
Sun-Ray Coal Co.	52 00				52 00	utilities			
Western Metropoly	317 25		317 25						
Murray Bakery	117 00		117 00						
Gay Meyda Laundry	47 00				47 00	direct expense			
Murray Grocers	167 50		167 50						
Litchenglen Co.	22 80				22 80	supplies			
North Hall Grocery	212 30		212 30						
State Insurance Co.	380 00						380 00	prepaid insurance	
City of Chicago	25 00				25 00	food license			
Wauer Milk Co.	32 50		32 50						
Kentucky Distillers	73 00			73 00					
TOTALS									

DAILY REPORT — FORM NO. 4

It is usually more convenient to note the sales and cash receipts information used in the Sales and Cash Receipts — Form No. 1 on a daily summary sheet, since this can be filled out at the cashier's stand where the cash is counted and the deposit made up, where the registers are read, or where the guests' checks are totaled. Then at a later and more convenient time the information can be transcribed on Form No. 1.

This daily summary can be made on a plain sheet of memorandum paper, of course, or it can be amplified, as is illustrated in Form No. 4, to the point where it shows the sales by meals, sales taxes collected, the covers served, the detail of charge sales and collections on accounts receivable, the detail of cash paid out of drawer, and such things as the bank deposit, the bank balance, and the accounts receivable balance.

In some of the larger restaurants the daily report also shows the weather, the daily food and payroll costs, and the sales by dining rooms or types of service.

A simple memorandum for a small restaurant might, for instance, contain only the following information:

1. Date and Day		Mon. April 3,19--
2. Cash On Hand At End of Day		$324.35
3. Less Beginning Change Fund		100.00
4. Balance to be Deposited		$224.35
5. Cash Paid Out of Drawer,		
Postage	$5.00	
Potatoes	5.15	10.15
6. Total Cash Sales For The Day		$234.50

In this case it is assumed that all sales are for cash and that only food is sold, the simplest type of operation. Daily Report — Form No. 4 was devised to cover the needs of the owner of a medium sized restaurant who desires to know more about his sales and customers and whose operation includes food, beverage, and cigar stand sales, and who occasionally extends credit to a customer and controls his sales by means of a cash register or by the use of guest checks or both.

The day and date are included in the heading for each day.

FOOD AND BEVERAGE SALES

The food and beverage sales section of the report provides a column for the register readings and another for the dollar amount of the sales. Then, an additional column is provided for the count of food customers served.

By reading the registers at the close of each meal period and deducting the previous reading, it is possible to obtain the sales for each meal. We advocate that the registers be read by someone other than the cashier on duty, since these registers act as a control on her work. Usually the food and beverage sales can be recorded on separate keys in the register, or there may be a separate register at the bar.

If the register is at the cashier's stand it may also have a counter for the number of persons served. Otherwise, it would probably be necessary to use and total the guests' checks to obtain the meal count each day and, if desired, for each meal period.

If some customers are allowed to charge their meals and pay later, a memorandum should be made of the date, the amount, and the name of the person who owes the money. If a guest check is used, it is usually more convenient to have the guest sign it. In all instances these charges must be included in the sales either by being rung upon the register or being counted with the other guest checks on which cash has been paid. As stated in the text on Form No. 1 — Sales and Cash Receipts, it is advisable to have a convenient means of listing the charge sales and accounts receivable collections. A form of such detailed record is shown on the reverse side of the Daily Report — Form No. 4. This reverse side provides for the name and amount, the amount of tip, or any fee on collections.

Sales taxes are accounted for on a separate key in some cash registers; when they are not, the cashier usually sets the amount collected for sales taxes aside to be accounted for and separated from sales at the close of her shift.

Cigar stand sales might also be accounted for separately in this same manner.

CASH SUMMARY

The next section of the daily report is concerned with the cash summary for the day. Beginning with the food and beverage sales taken from the registers or guest checks, all cash taken in on sales tax, cigar stand, tips charged, collections of accounts receivable and miscellaneous receipts — such as vending machine or telephone commissions, waste sales, etc., is added to arrive at a total of sales and cash receipts. The amount of cash paid out of drawer and the meals charged on credit are deducted from this total, and the result is the net cash receipts to be accounted for.

Meanwhile, the cashier has counted the cash on hand at the close of the day and has deducted the change fund supplied at the beginning of the day, leaving the amount to be deposited. This deposit should equal the cash receipts to be accounted. Any difference will be an overage or shortage in the cash, shown on the last line of this report form.

ACCOUNTS RECEIVABLE

To complete the daily report, a section has been provided in which to summarize the charge account transactions for the day. To yesterday's balance of uncollected accounts, today's charges are added and today's collections or allowances are deducted to arrive at the total of uncollected receivables at the end of the day. Allowances or adjustments of accounts receivable are sometimes necessary as a matter of policy or to reflect the cost of commissions to credit card agencies. It may also sometimes be necessary to write an account off as uncollectible. These allowances must be journalized by the bookkeeper at the end of the month to keep the accounts receivable from customers in balance. The practical entry for allowances in a small operation would be to charge these write-offs and adjustments to "Administrative and General Expense" and to credit "Customers Accounts Receivable."

BANK BALANCE

A space is also provided to show the daily bank balance. This balance is obtained by the following formula: to the bank balance of yesterday add today's deposit as shown in the cash summary, and deduct the total of today's checks drawn on this account as taken from Cash Disbursements—Form No. 2.

The remainder of this daily report form provides a space in which to detail the cash paid out of the drawer. In this space should be recorded the name of the payee, a description of the item paid for, and the amount paid. It is advisable to use a small petty cash voucher as a memorandum for such payments. These forms are standard at most stationers and provide for the date, name, description of item paid for and the amount paid as well as a space for the name of the person receiving the money.

With a daily report or cash summary form the gathering of the daily information on sales and cash receipts can be systematized to the point where it is a relatively easy matter and takes only a few minutes at some convenient time during the day. It is for this reason that this particular form has been included as an illustration in this section of the book.

In illustration of the use of the forms, specimen transactions are shown so that the small restaurant operator can see how these four forms make up a complete and adequate set of records for his daily transactions.

DAILY REPORT

DAY _Friday_

DATE _April 3,_ 19___

SUMMARY OF SALES

	REGISTER READING	FOOD FOOD SALES	CUSTOMERS SERVED	BEVERAGE REGISTER READING	BEVERAGE SALES
YESTERDAY'S READING	10,124 80			6,483 30	
BREAKFAST	10,211 30	86 50	144		
LUNCH	10,504 55	293 25	245	6,576 10	92 80
DINNER	10,701 40	196 85	81	6,626 55	50 45
BANQUETS AND PARTIES		none			none
TOTAL SALES		576 60	470		143 25

CASH SUMMARY	AMOUNTS		ACCOUNTS RECEIVABLE	AMOUNTS	
FOOD SALES	576 60		BALANCE YESTERDAY	222 45	
BEVERAGE SALES	143 25		TODAY'S CHARGES	32 80	
CIGAR STAND	14 00		TOTAL	255 25	
SALES TAXES	22 00		TODAY'S COLLECTIONS	4 65	
TIPS CHARGED	5 00		ALLOWANCES	18 00	22 65
COLLECTED ACCOUNTS	4 65		BALANCE TODAY		232 60
OTHER RECEIPTS			BANK BALANCE		
Illinois Bell - Comm.	6 00		BALANCE YESTERDAY	6,872 20	
			TODAY'S DEPOSIT	730 90	
			TOTAL	7,603 10	
TOTAL RECEIPTS	771 50		CHECKS DRAWN	1,623 78	
DEDUCT			BALANCE TODAY	5,979 32	
TIPS PAID OUT	5 00		PETTY CASH PAID OUTS TODAY		
CASH PAID OUTS	2 25				
ACCOUNTS CHARGED	32 80		NAME	ITEM	AMOUNT
TOTAL DEDUCTIONS	40 05		Joe Wintersmith	window washing	2 25
NET CASH RECEIPTS	731 45				
CASH IN DRAWER	855 90				
DEDUCT CHANGE FUND	125 00				
CASH DEPOSIT	730 90				
CASH-OVER OR (SHORT)	(55)		TOTAL CASH PAID OUTS	2 25	

(Front Side)

117

DAILY REPORT

DAY _Friday_   DATE _April 3,_ 19___

CUSTOMER'S ACCOUNTS CHARGED

CHECK NUMBER	NAME	TOTAL AMOUNT CHARGED	TIPS CHARGED
2418	George Hoyland	15 60	2 00
2472	Harry B. Smith	17 20	3 00
TOTAL ACCOUNTS CHARGED		32 80	5 00

CUSTOMER'S ACCOUNTS COLLECTED

NAME	AMOUNT PAID	COLLECTION FEE	TOTAL ACCOUNT
Raymond Mansfield	4 65		4 65
TOTAL ACCOUNTS COLLECTED	4 65		4 65

ALLOWANCES

NAME	REASON FOR ALLOWANCE	AMOUNT
Jacob Ascher	bad debt	18 00
TOTAL ALLOWANCES		18 00

(Reverse Side)

PAYROLL RECORDS—FORMS NO. 5 AND NO. 6

Because of the record keeping requirements of the Fair Labor Standards Act, which was amended to include restaurants under the jurisdiction of the Federal Department of Labor as of February 1, 1967, it was deemed advisable to outline a sample payroll sheet and employment card for the guidance of the smaller restaurant operator. As stated earlier in this text, these two forms are not included as final, but rather to be used as a guide based upon today's experience and to alert the smaller restaurant operator to prepare for the time when he may come under the jurisdiction of the Wage and Hour Law.

Since most restaurants, and particularly the smaller ones, are on a weekly payroll basis the Payroll Sheet—Form No. 5 has been designed accordingly. Where salaries and wages are paid semi-monthly or monthly the columns outlined can easily be adapted to this policy of payment.

There are many payroll systems and stock forms of payroll sheets and employment cards available at printing and stationery houses which may better fit the needs in some cases. The main purpose of the forms outlined here is to indicate how the essential elements making up the payroll cost can be compiled to indicate compliance with the Wage and Hour Law, which requirements and rulings to date are outlined in a later section of this book.

The forms are so designed that the record plan can be adapted to a system whereby the payroll check, payroll sheet and employment record can be made out simultaneously with one entry, since this is probably the type of payroll record that will be most commonly used. The main purpose of the illustrations is to indicate the type of payroll information that will be required in the event of an examination by the Wage and Hour Division.

PAYROLL SHEET—FORM NO. 5

This form anticipates that a separate payroll bank account will be used, and the totals in the illustration are tied into the amounts shown in the Cash Disbursements—Form No. 2—where the payroll account reimbursement check is illustrated.

As suggested in the Cash Disbursements Form, the payroll checks should be entered in numerical order as they are drawn and each given a separate line on the payroll sheet. It is also suggested that, if possible, the payroll should be lined up so that each class of employees is grouped together, using a classification similar to that illustrated in Schedule G-1 of PART II in this book.

The columns on the payroll sheet are listed as follows:

	Column Number
Name	
Position	
Hours Worked	1
Hourly Rate	2
Total Payroll	3
Distributed Tips and Service Charges	4
Total Paid by Employer	5

	Column Number
Memo Only { Employees' Meals	6
Reported Tips	7
Wage and Hour Total	8
Employee Deductions { F.I.C.A.	9
Income Tax	10
Other (Coded)	11
Total Deductions	12
Net Pay	13
Check Number	14

The payroll sheet will indicate at the top the weeks covered. The columns for the name of the employee and the position held were not numbered as they do not enter into the payroll computation.

COLUMN 1 — HOURS WORKED
COLUMN 2 — HOURLY RATE

The hours worked and the wage rate are entered in Columns (1) and (2), respectively. The time record will be taken from a time card or a book kept by the department head, and you will note that in the illustration we contemplated a six-day, 48-hour week for male employees and supervisors, and a five-day, 40-hour week for waitresses. Also, the wage rate for tipped employees, set at 75 cents per hour, considered the 50% credit in meeting the minimum wage requirement.

COLUMN 3 — TOTAL PAYROLL

Hours worked multiplied by the hourly wage rate is the amount of cash payroll expense of the employer and this total is entered in Column (3).

COLUMN 4 — DISTRIBUTED TIPS AND SERVICE CHARGES

The amount of tips or service charges collected by the employer on banquet checks, etc. and that is distributed to the employee is shown in Column (4).

COLUMN 5 — TOTAL PAID BY EMPLOYER

The payroll expense, plus the tips and service charges collected and distributed by the employer, shown in Column (5), is the gross amount due to the employee for services rendered. The net amount of the payroll check is arrived at by taking the employee deductions from this gross figure.

COLUMN 6 — EMPLOYEE MEALS
COLUMN 7 — REPORTED TIPS

Columns (6) and (7) are memorandums only and contain information needed to indicate compliance with the minimum wage law and the amounts to be used in computing withholding for Federal Income Taxes and F.I.C.A. taxes.

The value used in the illustration for employees' meals was 25 cents per meal, which is the arbitrary value used in Illinois for payroll tax purposes. While it is true that a different, and probably higher, valuation may be used in meeting Federal Minimum Wage requirements, this will probably not be computed unless it is necessary to prove compliance, and in the illustrations for Form No. 5 the wage rates used obviate this necessity.

For federal income tax purposes tipped employees are supposed to report to the employer the amount of tips they have received direct from the customers, which amounts are considered in determining withholding taxes. This becomes doubly important in connection with the up to 50% credit allowance in computing compliance with the Fair Labor Standards Act. With a weekly payroll it would be more practical to have the employee report weekly, as indicated in the illustrations used.

COLUMN NO. 8—WAGE AND HOUR TOTAL

The total paid by the employer, plus the credits for employee meals and reported tips, is the amount indicating compliance with the Wage and Hour Law.

It is also the payroll amount used in computing F.I.C.A. taxes and federal withholding taxes subject to the provision of the Internal Revenue Service in regard to meals furnished employees for the benefit of the employer. On such meals the employee is not required, at present, to pay federal income tax.

DEDUCTIONS

In Form No. 5 columns are provided for the withholding of the employees payroll and income taxes. A third column is provided, with a space for a code number, for any other payroll deductions, such as group insurance, union dues, cash advances, etc. In cases where there are deductions of a weekly recurring nature that would affect the employees "take-home" pay, it may be more practical to provide additional columns to cover them. However, in the illustration on Form No. 5, each type of other deduction is indicated by a code number and the total is recapped at the bottom of the payroll sheet under Column (11).

COLUMN 9—F.I.C.A.

The employees' portion of the Federal Insurance Contribution Act taxes was computed at the 1967 rate of 4.4%.

COLUMN 10—INCOME TAX

The amount withheld by the employer for the employees' Federal Income Taxes was computed on the basis of 1967 tables, using an assumed number of exemptions as they might have applied.

COLUMN 11—OTHER DEDUCTIONS
COLUMN 12—TOTAL DEDUCTIONS

Columns for other deductions from employees' wages and the total deductions in determining the employees' "take-home" pay are provided to facilitate the computations of net pay.

COLUMN 13—NET PAY

The gross amount shown in Column (5) less the total deductions shown in Column (12) results in the "net pay," which is the amount of the payroll check to be issued to the employee for the week under consideration.

COLUMN 14—CHECK NUMBER

The check number is shown in the last column for practical purposes in making up bank reconciliations, auditing, etc.

GENERAL

Form No. 5 contains eight illustrations of payroll entries which were varied to indicate how this weekly payroll sheet would be used to provide the information probably most needed in connection with the Wage and Hour Law. Also at the bottom of this payroll sheet the total payroll for the week is illustrated, with a check mark indicating the posting to the Cash Disbursements—Form No. 2—covering the reimbursement check to the payroll account and, at the same time, getting the payroll expense into the general records through the entry in the Disbursements Record.

The payroll sheet may also serve as a control of payroll if the checks are written by departments, or position classes. Thus, at the time the payroll is completed an analysis of time worked by departments can be extracted, which, when compared with the sales volume or number of meals served, could disclose areas in which productivity has dropped or possible other distortions in wages.

PAYROLL SHEET
Week Ending 4/5/

Name	Position	Hours Worked	Hourly Rate	Total Payroll	Distributed Tips & Ser. Charge	Total Paid by Employer	Memo Only Employee Meals	Memo Only Reported Tips	Wage & Hour Total	FICA	Income Tax	Deductions Other Code	Deductions Other Amount	Total Deduction	Net Pay	Check Number
John Q Adams	Manager	42	5.00	240.00		240.00	4.50		240.50	10.76	33.40	(1)	6.00	50.17	189.83	785
Carl Davis	Cook	48	2.00	96.00		96.00	3.00		99.00	4.36	7.70	(1)	6.00	19.06	77.94	786
Mary Martin	Hostess	48	1.00	48.00	20.00	68.00	3.00	50.00	121.00	5.32	17.50	(1)	6.00	28.82	39.18	787
John Cook	Dishwasher	48	1.50	72.00		72.00	3.00		75.00	3.30	6.10	(2)	10.00	19.40	52.60	788
Nora Brown	Waitress	40	.75	30.00	7.00	37.00	2.50	45.00	84.50	3.72	9.70	(1)	6.00	19.42	17.58	789
Ruth Smith	Waitress	16	.75	12.00		12.00	1.00	20.00	33.00	1.45	4.10			5.55	6.45	790
Rita Tiek	Waitress	40	.75	30.00	10.00	40.00	2.50	50.00	92.50	4.07	11.20	(1)	6.00	21.27	18.73	791
Betty Young	waitress	6	.75	4.50		4.50	.50	15.00	20.00	.88	2.20			3.08	1.42	792
TOTAL Payroll To Form No.2 (✓)				3000.00 (✓)	100.00 (✓)	3100.00	105.00	725.00	3930.00 (✓)	172.92 (✓)	575.00 (✓)		140.00 (✓)	887.92	2212.08 (✓)	

RECAP. (✓)

CODE NO.
(1) INSURANCE 120.00
(2) EMPLOYEE ADVANCE 20.00
TOTAL. 140.00

123

EMPLOYMENT RECORD – FORM NO. 6

The employment record, Form No. 6, is designed to become a permanent record of the employees' annual earnings, and it will be one of the major records required in cases involving disputes regarding minimum wages and other employee-employer relationships. As such, this employment record should contain as much information as it is practical to insert on the face of the form.

The following items should therefore be shown on this form.

1. Employee's full name
2. Social security number
3. Most recent address
4. Telephone number
5. Department or type of work
6. Sex
7. Date of birth
8. Employee number, if used
9. Number of exemptions for withholding tax purposes
10. Date of employment
11. Hourly rate of pay and space for any rate changes with the date
12. Date of termination
13. Reason for termination
14. Nearest relative and address – Name and address of person to notify in case of an emergency.
15. Computation of employee meal credit.

Other information that will supplement the Employment Record such as the employees' job application form, withholding certificate, record of employees' tips and time cards or time book should be maintained for each employee. While we do not illustrate these various forms in this portion of the Uniform System of Accounts for Restaurants, they are readily obtainable from stationery stores and the U. S. Government Printing Office.

The example form has been designed to be used with a one-write system along with the Payroll Sheet – Form No. 5, to accumulate quarterly and end of calendar year earnings for the reporting of individual wages to federal and state agencies. For example, illustration on Form 6, John Q. Adams has earned during the first quarter $3,700 for the purposes of Wage and Hour totals. In this manner the employer is able to maintain a cumulative total for the purposes of determining the tax liability for federal and state unemployment taxes and that under the Federal Insurance Contributions Act.

Under the Wage and Hour Law, the credit for employees' meals could become a substantial factor in complying with the minimum hourly wage. This is explained in greater detail in Appendix D; however, the method and the amount used to determine this credit should be reflected on Form No. 6. Thus, any inspection of the employee records by governmental agencies will be eased and complete compliance with the various regulations can easily be determined.

EMPLOYMENT RECORD

Name: John Q. Adams   Sec. Sec. No. 376-28-7664   Address 1301 N. Main St., Anytown, USA 00631   Phone 531-6672

Dept. or Place of Work: Restaurant Manager   Emp. No. 22   Hr. Rate 5.00

Sex: ☐ Male ☐ Female   Date 1/1   Meal Credit: 2 Meals Daily at 25¢ per meal

Birth Date: June 3, 1931

Income Tax Status

No. of Exempts. 3   Effective Date January 1   Date of Exem. Cert. January 1

Name	Emp. No.	Period Ending	Time Worked	Earnings Regular	Dist. Tips	Total	Employee Meals	Reported Tips	Wage & Hour Total	FICA	Income Tax	Fixed Deductions	Deductions Other	Total	Net Pay	Check No.	Total	Cumulative Earnings	Pct.
																			1
																			2
																			3
																			4
																			13
																			14
Total 1st Quarter				3000.00	300.00	3300.00	60.00	340.00	3700.00	162.80	470.00		3000.00	932.80	2367.20	Total		3700.00	
																Year To Date			
John Q. Adams		4/6/	49 hrs	240.00	24.00	264.00	4.50		244.50	10.76	33.40 (1)		6.00	50.17	189.83	785		3944.50	1
																			2
																			3
																			4
																			13
																			14
																Total			
																Year To Date			

Date Employed   Date Terminated   Reason for Termination   Date Re-Employed

Spouse   Person to notify in emergency

APPENDIX A

FOOD COST CONTROL

This section is written primarily for the smaller restaurant operator who is not in a position to maintain any extensive food control system and yet may want some idea of what his food costs may be from day to day.

The larger restaurants have an office staff and executives who perform and follow these control functions based on a system designed to meet their requirements. It would not be practical to describe these controls in detail in this text, and it is advisable that professional help be obtained in setting up and using these more detailed and elaborate control systems.

Even in the smallest of operations, however, a daily cumulative summary of sales, food cost, and the cost ratio to sales will be found extremely helpful. An outlining of the method of obtaining these daily facts is the purpose of this Appendix A.

PURCHASING, RECEIVING, STORING, PREPARATION

No control system has yet been devised which, by means of the paper work alone, will bring about the desired results. Food control is not only a clerical function but it also calls for close attention on the part of the management and the crew to proper purchasing, receiving, storing, preparation, production costs, and merchandising. The preparation of daily cost figures through a food control system serves as a guide to those in charge and enables them to take corrective steps when the costs fluctuate too sharply and are out of line.

Because of the importance of proper purchasing, receiving, storing, preparation and production control in every restaurant operation, a brief discussion of these functions should precede any consideration of control procedures.

PURCHASING

Stated simply, efficient purchasing is the obtaining of the quality of merchandise desired at the most favorable price. To accomplish this it is necessary to know food in order that the grade, size, weight, pack and quality most suitable to the particular restaurant operation may be specified.

Competitive bids are advisable where the restaurant owner is in a position to obtain them and, in this connection, established specifications are again important. Overbuying should be avoided and the contracting for future deliveries is not recommended.

As prefabricated or "ready-foods" are becoming increasingly available and are being more and more extensively used, purchase specifications should be established for these items.

RECEIVING

Proper checking of the quality, weight, and count of merchandise when it is delivered is probably the most frequently ignored of all of the rules of good control and yet it is the most important.

Adequate scales should be available and, if it is at all possible, the authority to receipt for merchandise should be limited to one trustworthy person. It is not good business to allow anyone in the kitchen to sign for

126

deliveries or to permit the delivery man to place his merchandise in the stock room or coolers without first checking it in. Both of these circumstances invite losses and increased costs.

The control of merchandise is much more efficient if a daily receiving record is kept on all deliveries and if requisition forms are used for all goods withdrawn from the storeroom. These records can be obtained at most hotel and restaurant stationers, who carry them in stock form.

STORING

Merchandise should be stored promptly after it is accepted. The storage areas should be kept clean and orderly. Old merchandise should be moved to the front so that the "first in — first out" practice can be followed.

The temperatures of the coolers should be checked frequently to protect the contents. Locks should be provided for all storage areas.

Inventories should be taken at each month-end. A bound split-leaf inventory book which provides for twelve consecutive inventories with a single listing of the items, is recommended and this can also be obtained in stock forms from any stationer.

PREPARATION

Merchandise should be prepared in moderate quantities and as near to the time it is to be served as possible. Advance preparation not only results in the deterioration in the quality and appearance of the products but also in substantial direct losses

PRODUCTION CONTROL

The quantities of the various menu items to be prepared should be predetermined and recorded for the guidance of the respective kitchen employees.

This record should also be used to note the quantities which remain unsold so as to minimize future production of these items in excess of existing demands.

CONTROL PROCEDURES

In the case of a small restaurant where there is no storeroom to control and the proprietor does not use a receiving sheet or requisitions, a very simple daily summary of sales and costs may suffice as a guide to food costs. This information can be placed on a columnar sheet with a line devoted to each day's transactions, as illustrated in the following table:

	Sales		Food Purchases		Food Cost Ratio	
Date	Today	To-Date	Today	To-Date	Today	To-Date
1	$250.75		$110.17		43.94%	
2	301.05	$ 551.80	131.86	$ 242.03	43.80	43.86%
3	298.80	850.60	155.55	397.58	52.06	46.74
4	360.10	1,210.70	172.22	569.80	47.83	47.06
5	328.95	1,539.65	113.47	683.27	34.49	44.38
6	388.65	1,928.30	207.54	890.81	53.40	46.20

	Sales		Food Purchases		Food Cost Ratio	
Date	Today	To-Date	Today	To-Date	Today	To-Date
29	344.40	8,492.25	152.13	3,772.11	44.17	44.42
30	319.60	8,811.85	130.11	3,902.22	40.71	44.28
31	322.15	9,134.00	109.08	4,011.30	33.86	43.92
Monthly Total		$9,134.00		$4,011.30		43.92%
Add Beginning Inventory				856.54		xx xx
Total				$4,867.84		xx xx
Less Ending Inventory				982.62		xx xx
Net Cost of Food for the Month				$3,855.22		42.54%

It is obvious that where each day's purchases are considered as the cost, the ratio of cost to sales may fluctuate rather widely from day to day. However, the cumulative to-date cost ratio becomes a fairly accurate barometer, provided that the food inventory is maintained at a reasonably uniform level.

Wherever it is possible, requisitions for supplies from the storeroom should be mandatory. Even then it is usually necessary to charge out certain items as they are purchased. These are referred to as "direct purchases" and include any merchandise that must be delivered immediately to the preparation department. The extent of such direct purchases depends largely on the location of the coolers. If these are in the kitchen it is likely that all food except staple items would be charged directly to operations when they are purchased.

If a receiving sheet and requisitions for items issued from a food storeroom are used, a columnar sheet headed in the manner shown in Form No. 7 — Summary of Food Costs and Sales is recommended as a simplified daily control.

The use of this form requires that a receiving record be maintained, whereby separate totals of purchases charged to the storeroom and of direct charges to the kitchen are provided. It also requires the use of requisitions for withdrawals from the storeroom. These must be cost-priced, extended and totaled.

This form can be better illustrated in the table which follows:

Column Number		Amounts	
1.	Storeroom Inventory at Beginning	$1,120.33	
2.	Storeroom Purchases	125.05	
3.	Total	$1,245.38	
4.	Storeroom Issues	110.12	$110.12
	Line 2 — Column 1 — New Storeroom Figure	$1,135.26	
5.	Direct Purchases		187.57
6.	Total Cost		$297.69
7.	Deduct: Transfers to Beverages		2.10
8.	Net Food Cost Today		$295.59
9.	Net Food Cost To-Date		–
10.	Food Sales Today		$675.50
11.	Food Sales To-Date		–
12.	Cost Ratio to Sales Today		43.76%
13.	Cost Ratio to Sales To-Date		–

The fluctuation in the to-date food cost ratio is used as an indication of the efficiency of the restaurant operation. The immediate investigation of the causes for any unusual increase in that figure often brings about prompt correction and improved results.

Some restaurant men want to go even further into their costs and do so by dividing their purchases into major groups or categories, by means of which the individual group cost ratios to sales can be determined.

The following illustrates three such methods of distribution, in varying degree of detail, which were observed in reviewing restaurant statements in connection with the preparation of this book.

ANALYSIS OF FOOD PURCHASES

METHOD A		METHOD B		METHOD C	
Divisions	Item	Divisions	Item	Divisions	Item
1.	Meats Poultry	1.	Meats	1.	Beef
				2.	Veal
				3.	Lamb or Mutton
				4.	Pork
		2.	Poultry	5.	Poultry
2.	Fish	3.	Fish	6.	Seafood
3.	Produce	4.	Vegetables	7.	Vegetables
4.	Staples			8.	Salads and Relishes
		5.	Fruits	9.	Fruits
		6.	Groceries	10.	Eggs
				11.	Cheese
		7.	Butter	12.	Butter
				13.	Dining Room Groceries
				14.	Dining Room Butter
				15.	Shortening and Oil
				16.	Coffee, Tea, Cocoa
				17.	Staples
5.	Milk & Cream	8.	Milk & Cream	18.	Milk & Cream
6.	Bread & Rolls	9.	Bakery	19.	Bake Shop
				20.	Pastry Shop
7.	Ice Cream	10.	Ice Cream	21.	Ice Cream

These three illustrations of how food purchases might be classified show that the extent of the analysis of purchases depends on the judgment of the restaurant man on the value that the detail compiled may be to him in watching these costs.

In a purchase analysis of this type it is suggested that a four-column sheet be used each month. The first two columns show (1) the distribution of the purchases for the current month and (2) the year-to-date totals. The second two columns show the ratio of each item to food sales for the current month (3) and for the year-to-date (4).

In smaller operations where the day's purchases may closely approximate the cost of food it is possible to use in place of the Summary of Food Cost and Sales the following Form No. 8 Daily Food Costs Based on Total Purchases to serve as a dual purpose receiving record — purchase (food cost) analysis report.

In using this form each invoice should be identified by vendor's name, number and total amount.

129

The amount of each invoice, representing a purchase made, should then be distributed according to categories listed as columnar headings, and the various categories should be totaled.

Once all purchases have been totaled and decreased by the value of possible "Transfers to Bar" the "Total Cost Today" is to be shown under the "Total Invoice" heading. When this total is established, the cost (purchase) components should also be shown under the applicable commodity cost totals and they should be balanced to the previously established total purchase (food) cost of the day.

By adding the "Today" cost figures in all columns to those recorded for the preceding day or days, the "Total Cost To-Date" is established.

By dividing the total cost, as well as all its component costs, into the sales figures for the corresponding period. The over-all food cost percentage as well as the various component commodity cost ratios will become known.

If the total food cost ratio should increase, that increase will be reflected in one or more of the commodity cost ratios shown in the distribution and this will indicate where attention should be directed and corrective action taken.

SUMMARY OF FOOD COST AND SALES
FOR MONTH OF _April_ 19__

DATE	(1) STOREROOM INVENTORY AT BEGINNING	(2) STOREROOM PURCHASES	(3) TOTAL	(4) STOREROOM ISSUES	(5) DIRECT PURCHASES	(6) TOTAL COST	(7) DEDUCT TRANSFERS TO BEVERAGE	(8) NET FOOD COST TODAY	(9) NET FOOD COST TO-DATE	(10) FOOD SALES TODAY	(11) FOOD SALES TO-DATE	(12) COST RATIO TO SALES TODAY	(13) COST RATIO TO SALES TO-DATE
1	1,120.33	125.05	1,245.38	110.12	187.57	297.69	2.10	295.59	—	675.50	—	43.76	—
2	1,135.26	87.30	1,222.56	122.71	137.76	260.47	.90	259.57	555.16	612.10	1,287.60	42.41	43.12
3	1,099.85												
4													
5													
6													
7													
8													
9													
10													
18													
19													
20													
21													
22													
23													
24													
25													
26													
27													
28													
29													
30													
31													
TOTALS													

131

DAILY FOOD COSTS BASED ON TOTAL PURCHASES

DAY Monday
DATE October 1, 19

SALES TODAY: $1200
SALES TO DATE: $1200

VENDOR	INVOICE #	TOTAL INVOICE	BEEF	OTHER MEATS POULTRY	SEAFOOD	PRODUCE	STAPLES	DAIRY	BREAD ROLLS
Smith Provision	1102	150 00	85 00	40 00	25 00				
Land O Lot	301	15 00						15 00	20 00
Baker Products	703	40 00					20 00		
Easy Way Flour	26	19 00					19 00		
Milbra Produce	C-16	48 70				48 70			
ABC Poultry	806	38 00		38 00					
Soda Bread	7856	18 50							18 50
Burki	416	22 50			6 00	16 50			
Meat Supply	15618	110 00	15 00	95 00					
TOTAL PURCHASES TODAY		461 70	100 00	173 00	31 00	65 20	39 00	15 00	38 50
LESS: TRANSFERS TO BAR									
TOTAL COST TODAY		461 70	100 00	123 00	31 00	65 20	39 00	15 00	38 50
TOTAL COST TO DATE									
COST PERCENTAGE TO DATE		38 48	8 33	14 42	2 58	5 43	3 26	1 26	3 21

132

APPENDIX B

BEVERAGE COST CONTROL

Just as with the proper recording of food costs, the restaurant man should know how his beverage cost ratios are maintained from day to day, or, at least, from week to week.

The control of beverages can best be accomplished by setting up a separate control on the stock rooms and the bar.

The stock room, or wine room, should be kept securely locked at all times and only one person should have access to it for the purpose of storing and issuing the merchandise. Requisitions should be required for all merchandise issued and it is desirable that these be written in duplicate so that the bottles issued can be checked by the bartender against his copy.

A perpetual inventory record should be maintained on every item in the stock room so that the physical counts at the end of each month can be compared with the balances shown on the respective account cards. Any differences should be immediately investigated. These perpetual inventory records permit the spot-checking of the count of any item during the month, if desired.

Form No. 9 – Summary of Beverage Costs and Sales illustrates the daily and cumulative to-date cost and sales summary for the bar operation. In order that the daily cost will approximate as nearly as possible the actual cost of merchandise consumed, it is advisable to establish a par stock of each item at the bar and to replace the empty bottles daily. In this manner the daily issue to the bar will restore the stock to the par level, and it will also substantially represent the merchandise sold on the preceding day.

Form 9 is illustrated in table form as follows:

Column Number		Amounts
1.	Wine Room Issues	$26.20
2.	Food Transfers to Bar	2.10
3.	Total Cost Today	$28.30
4.	Total Cost To-Date	–
5.	Beverage Sales Today	87.75
6.	Beverage Sales To-Date	–
7.	Cost Ratio to Sales Today	32.25%
8.	Cost Ratio to Sales To-Date	–

Some bars are controlled by calculating the sales value of the daily issues to the bar and thus arriving at a daily and monthly overage and shortage as compared with the actual bar sales. This is done by calculating the number of drinks per bottle issued, based on the standard sizes of drinks sold, multiplied by their beverage list prices. This is a control that needs the advice and assistance of someone familiar with beverage cost control procedures if it is to be made effective, and it is advisable to have professional services in setting up and using this type of control.

Some operators are content to make a simple division of sales and costs into a few major categories such as:

    Mixed Drinks and Cocktails
    Beer and Ale
    Wines
    Soft Drinks
    Bottle Sales

The profit potential on each of these divisions of beverage sales is different and it depends on the size of the drink and the prices charged. Thus, the total costs may be affected by the fluctuation in the proportion of sales in each group.

Some go even farther in their distribution as may be evidenced in the following list taken from a daily beverage control report in use by a large restaurant:

ITEM	BY THE BOTTLE			BY THE GLASS		
	Cost	Sales	%	Cost	Sales	%
Champagne — Imported	$	$		$	$	
Champagne — Domestic						
Still Wine — Imported						
Still Wine — Domestic						
Whiskeys — Rye						
Bourbon						
Scotch						
Irish						
Gin						
Vodka						
Rum						
Brandy						
Vermouth						
Cordials						
Beer and Ale — Bottled						
Beer and Ale — Draught						
Non-alcoholic						
Waters and Mixing						
Bitters						
Syrups						
Carbonic Gas						
Bar Groceries						
Corkage						
TOTAL	$	$		$	$	

This form of report requires a detailed analysis of sales and is somewhat more involved than the other methods discussed in this text. It can be used only if all bar sales are recorded on checks and is therefore not adaptable for the average bar.

Regardless of the method employed, it is important that some form of control be established over even a small bar operation.

DESIGNED BY HORWATH & HORWATH

SUMMARY OF BEVERAGE COST AND SALES
FOR MONTH OF _April_ 19___

FORM 9

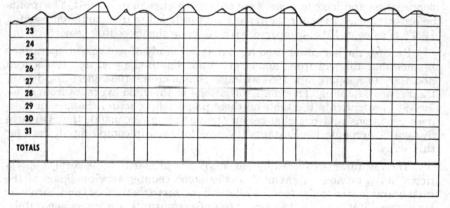

DATE	(1) BEVERAGE ISSUES	(2) FOOD TRANSFERS	(3) BEVERAGE COST TODAY	(4) BEVERAGE COST TO-DATE	(5) BEVERAGE SALES TODAY	(6) BEVERAGE SALES TO-DATE	(7) COST RATIO TO SALES TODAY	(8) COST RATIO TO SALES TO-DATE
1	26 20	2 10	28 30	—	87 25	—	32 25%	—
2	38 90	90	39 80	68 10	115 10	202 85	34 56	33 57%
3	42 20	1 90	44 10	112 20	130 55	333 40	33 78	33 65
4	39 75	2 40	42 15	154 35	119 60	453 00	35 24	34 07
5	34 70	2 10	36 80	191 15	112 05	565 05	32 85	33 83
6	(Sunday)							
7	41 50	75	42 25	233 40	124 20	689 25	34 02	33 86
8								
9								
10								
11								
23								
24								
25								
26								
27								
28								
29								
30								
31								
TOTALS								

APPENDIX C

THE EIGHTH ANNUAL STUDY
OF RESTAURANT OPERATIONS

Made by
Horwath & Horwath

Restaurants fared better in 1965 than in the preceding year but only because of a sharp increase in sales volume. For the 72 restaurants which contributed data to this study and represent many parts of the country, total food and beverage sales were 6% higher than in 1964 and profits before income taxes were up 7%. Thus, these restaurants had profits before income taxes of 4.2% of sales in 1965, compared with 4.1% in 1964.

The food cost per dollar sale was the same in both years, but the beverage cost per dollar sale showed a reduction. However, since the rise in controllable expenses exceeded the increase in sales, the profits before occupation costs, depreciation and income taxes were only 4% higher than in 1964. The profits before occupation costs for the restaurants included in this study represented 12.9% of sales in 1965, compared with 13.0% in the preceding year.

Because the sampling used for our latest study of restaurant operations is somewhat different from, and larger than, that used a year ago, it has been necessary to compute new 1964 averages, based on the 1964 operating data of the revised sampling. Therefore, variations in the 1965 averages from those for 1964 presented in the table on these pages reflect actual changes in business conditions and not changes in the sampling. As usual, the "Uniform System of Accounts for Restaurants" was followed in compiling all data for this study.

The restaurants covered by our study are primarily table-service operations, but a number of them also offer some counter service. Some of the restaurants serve only food, while others serve both food and alcoholic beverages. Statistics for the two types of restaurants are given separately, since we have found that all restaurants serving both food and beverages have similar operating problems, policies and patterns which tend to be different from those of restaurants which do not serve alcoholic beverages. As there are so many variations in the types of operation of restaurants serving only food, just one set of ratios representing the averages for all the "food only" restaurants is given.

The data for the restaurants serving both food and beverages, however, have been further broken down by location into the following groups:

Neighborhood—Situated in areas which are primarily residential but are near commercial concentrations providing an additional source of business.

Center City—Situated in the central business section of a city.

Suburban—Situated outside of a city.

A comparative summary of the ratios of profits before occupation costs to sales of the various categories of restaurants for the years 1965 and 1964 follows:

	1965	1964
Food only	14.7%	14.8%
Food and beverage		
Neighborhood	9.8%	9.5%
Center city	12.5	12.3
Suburban	14.6	15.6
Total	12.7%	12.8%
All restaurants	12.9%	13.0%

All groups of restaurants showed increases in sales volume in 1965 and all but the suburban restaurants selling both food and beverages recorded increases in the dollar amounts of profit available for rent, property taxes, property insurance, interest, depreciation and income taxes. In ratio to sales, however, only the neighborhood and center-city restaurants selling food and beverages showed improvements over 1964 in the profit before occupation costs.

The neighborhood restaurants, despite a gain of three-tenths of a point in 1965, again had the lowest ratio of profit before occupation costs of all the categories included in our study. The center-city restaurants also showed an increase, two-tenths of a point, over 1964 in the ratio of profit before occupation costs. On the other hand, the suburban restaurants serving both food and beverages not only showed a drop of a whole point in the ratio of profit before occupation costs but were the only ones to record a decrease dollarwise in profits from 1964. Nevertheless, the suburban restaurants had the second highest ratio of profit before occupation costs to sales in 1965.

"FOOD ONLY" RESTAURANTS MADE BEST SHOWING

The "food only" restaurants had the highest ratio of profit before occupation costs, although the 1965 ratio for this group was down one-tenth of a point from that of the preceding year. Since these restaurants cannot depend on high-profit beverage sales, they usually tend to take more advantage of the best controls and the newest methods, equipment, products and packaging offered in the restaurant field. Moreover, included in this group are several diner operations which are open 24 hours a day and have a heavy sales volume.

We have again carried our study only to the point of profit before occupation costs because these expenses vary according to differences in size, location, ownership and financing. However, we present below the 1965 ratios of occupation costs and depreciation to total sales for those restaurants contributing such data to our study:

		Food and Beverage		
	Food Only	Neighborhood	Center City	Suburban
Rent	5.1*%	5.1*%	5.6*%	8.3*%
Property taxes	1.0	.7*	.7*	.5*
Property insurance	.3	.4*	.2*	.3*
Interest	1.0*	.8*	.2*	.4*
Depreciation	3.4	3.0*	1.6*	2.1
Total	8.5%	7.6%	8.0*%	10.6%

*Average only of those restaurants reporting this item.

137

SUMMARY PROFIT AND LOSS STATEMENTS—EIGHTH ANNUAL STUDY

	All Restaurants	Food Only	Total	Food and Beverage Restaurants		
				Neighborhood	Center City	Suburban
SALES						
Food	78.1%	100.0%	75.6%	82.2%	74.4%	73.4%
Beverages	21.9		24.4	17.8	25.6	26.6
Total sales	100.0%	100.0%	100.0%	100.0%	100.0%	100.0%
COST OF SALES						
Food*	39.1%	37.7%	39.3%	44.0%	37.2%	39.2%
Beverages	29.3		29.3	35.7	27.9	28.9
Total cost of sales	36.9%	37.7%	36.8%	42.5%	34.8%	36.5%
GROSS PROFIT	63.1%	62.3%	63.2%	57.5%	65.2%	63.5%
OTHER INCOME	.9	.6	.9	1.1	.8	1.1
Total income	64.0%	62.9%	64.1%	58.6%	66.0%	64.6%
CONTROLLABLE EXPENSES						
Payroll	31.2%	31.7%	31.2%	29.4%	32.5%	30.3%
Employee benefits	3.5	3.5	3.5	2.9	4.0	3.2
Direct operating expenses	6.1	5.0	6.2	5.9	6.2	6.5
Music and entertainment	.7	.1	.8	.2	.7	1.3
Advertising and promotion	1.9	1.0	1.9	2.2	2.1	1.6
Utilities	1.8	2.5	1.7	1.8	1.8	1.6
Administrative and general	4.2	2.4	4.4	5.0	4.3	4.1
Repairs and maintenance	1.7	2.0	1.7	1.4	1.9	1.4
Total controllable expenses	51.1%	48.2%	51.4%	48.8%	53.5%	50.0%
PROFIT BEFORE OCCUPATION COSTS, DEPRECIATION AND INCOME TAXES	12.9%	14.7%	12.7%	9.8%	12.5%	14.6%

*Before credit for employees' meals

SUMMARY PROFIT AND LOSS STATEMENTS—SEVENTH ANNUAL STUDY

	All Restaurants	Food Only	Total	Food and Beverage Restaurants		
				Neighborhood	Center City	Suburban
SALES						
Food	78.0%	100.0%	75.6%	81.6%	75.2%	72.7%
Beverages	22.0		24.4	18.4	24.8	27.3
Total sales	100.0%	100.0%	100.0%	100.0%	100.0%	100.0%
COST OF SALES						
Food*	39.1%	37.0%	39.4%	44.2%	37.5%	39.0%
Beverages	30.1	.6	30.1	35.2	29.0	29.6
Total cost of sales	37.1%	37.0%	37.1%	42.5%	35.4%	36.4%
GROSS PROFIT	62.9%	63.0%	62.9%	57.5%	64.6%	63.6%
OTHER INCOME	.9	.6	.9	1.0	.8	1.0
Total income	63.8%	63.6%	63.8%	58.5%	65.4%	64.6%
CONTROLLABLE EXPENSES						
Payroll	31.4%	31.6%	31.4%	30.0%	32.7%	30.4%
Employee benefits	3.6	3.7	3.6	3.2	4.2	3.1
Direct operating expenses	6.0	5.1	6.1	5.7	6.1	6.4
Music and entertainment	.7	.1	.7	.3	.6	1.1
Advertising and promotion	1.9	1.0	1.9	2.2	2.0	1.7
Utilities	1.8	2.6	1.8	1.9	1.9	1.4
Administrative and general	3.8	2.9	3.9	4.3	3.8	3.5
Repairs and maintenance	1.6	1.8	1.6	1.4	1.8	1.4
Total controllable expenses	50.8%	48.8%	51.0%	49.0%	53.1%	49.0%
PROFIT BEFORE OCCUPATION COSTS, DEPRECIATION AND INCOME TAXES	13.0%	14.8%	12.8%	9.5%	12.3%	15.6%

*Before credit for employees' meals

For all the restaurants included in our study, the total dollar amount of occupation costs and depreciation was higher in 1965 than in the preceding year. However, the increase in sales and a decrease in the dollar charges for depreciation resulted in an improvement in the net profits before income taxes that was proportionately greater than the gain in sales.

A comparative summary of the ratios of profits before income taxes to sales for 1965 and 1964 follows:

	1965	1964
Food only	6.2%	6.4%
Food and beverage		
Neighborhood	2.2%	1.9%
Center City	4.6	4.2
Suburban	4.0	4.6
Total	4.0%	3.9%
All restaurants	4.2%	4.1%

While the ratio of profit before income taxes for the "food only" restaurants continued to be considerably higher than that of the restaurants selling both food and beverages, it is noteworthy that in 1965 the difference was slightly less than in the preceding year. If, in the face of rising merchandise and payroll costs, the "food only" restaurants in our sampling are to go on outperforming restaurants which serve both food and beverages, they will have to maintain tighter controls and take even greater advantage of good layout and equipment than in the past.

For all the restaurants covered by our study, food sales were up 6% in 1965 and beverage sales were 5% higher than in 1964. Thus, of each dollar of food and beverage income, 78.1% was from food sales and 21.9% from beverage sales in 1965, compared with 78.0% from food and 22.0% from beverages in the preceding year. Although in 1965 the beverage sales of the suburban restaurants represented a smaller proportion of total food and beverage income than in 1964, these restaurants, which usually enjoy a good dinner business, sold proportionately more beverages than the other two groups serving food and beverages.

FOOD AND BEVERAGE COSTS PER DOLLAR SALE

The over-all food cost per dollar sale, before credit for employees' meals, was the same in both 1965 and 1964, as increases in the food costs per dollar sale of the "food only" and suburban restaurants offset decreases in the food cost ratios of the neighborhood and center-city restaurants. The center-city restaurants also showed a decrease in the cost per dollar sale of beverages in 1965 as did the suburban restaurants, while the neighborhood restaurants recorded an increase in the beverage cost per dollar sale. As a result, the 1965 beverage cost per dollar sale of all restaurants serving both food and beverages was down from 1964 and the average gross profit of all the restaurants included in our study was better than in the preceding year.

140

TOTAL RESTAURANT PAYROLL UP 5%

According to our study, total restaurant payroll rose 5% in 1965, but an even greater increase in total food and beverage sales effected a decrease of two-tenths of a point in the ratio of payroll to total sales. Although the payrolls for all categories analyzed were higher, dollarwise, than in 1964, all but the "food only" restaurants recorded decreases in the ratios of payroll to total sales. Nevertheless, the center-city restaurants selling both food and beverages again spent the largest proportion of the income dollar on payroll.

The "prime cost," a combination of the costs of merchandise and payroll, is the most important expense ratio of the restaurant operation. For all the restaurants covered by our study, the ratio of the prime cost to sales was down four-tenths of a point from 1964. A comparative summary of the prime-cost ratios of the various categories of restaurants in our study for the years 1965 and 1964 follows:

	1965	1964
Food only	69.4%	68.6%
Food and beverage		
Neighborhood	71.9%	72.5%
Center-city	67.3	68.1
Suburban	66.8	66.8
Total	68.0%	68.5%
All restaurants	68.1%	68.5%

Despite a reduction of six-tenths of a point from 1964, the ratio of prime cost to sales for the neighborhood restaurants serving both food and beverages was the highest of all the groups in 1965, while that of the suburban restaurants, even though the same in both years, was the lowest. The center-city restaurants showed the greatest improvement, eight-tenths of a point, in the ratio of the prime cost to sales in 1965, while the "food only" restaurants recorded the only increase — one of eight-tenths of a point — over the preceding year.

OTHER CONTROLLABLE EXPENSES

The other controllable expenses for all the restaurants included in our study were higher than in 1964, but the ratios to sales of only direct operating, administrative and general and repairs and maintenance expenses reflected these rises. Because of the increase in sales, the ratios of music and entertainment, advertising and promotion, and utilities to sales showed no change in 1965, while that of employee benefits expense was down from the preceding year.

The direct operating expenses of the various restaurant categories rose proportionately more than sales in 1965, except in the "food only" restaurants, in which group the increase in sales effected a slight decrease in the ratio of these expenses to sales. In the following table we give a breakdown of the 1965 direct operating expenses so that restaurateurs can make more detailed comparative analyses of their figures:

141

	Food Only	Food and Beverage Neighborhood	Center City	Suburban
Laundry and linen and/or linen rental	.9%	1.5%	1.7%	1.8%
China, glassware and silver	.7	.5	1.2	.9
Cleaning and cleaning supplies	1.0	1.0	.7	1.3
Paper and guest supplies	1.4	.8	.4	.9
All other	1.0	2.1	2.2	1.6
Total	5.0%	5.9%	6.2%	6.5%

CONCLUSION

According to our study of restaurant operations, increases in sales in 1965 were not always sufficient to offset rises in expenses. Good volume should not cause a restaurant to relax controls over costs and expenses. Neither should competition, which undoubtedly affected the suburban restaurants in 1965, be accepted too readily as a reason for lowering profit margins.